Collins

Grand Designs
Abroad

Kevin McCloud & Kevin Telfer

Grand Designs
Abroad

Building your dream

Collins

First published in 2004 by Collins,
an imprint of HarperCollinsPublishers
77–85 Fulham Palace Road
London W6 8JB

The Collins website address is www.collins.co.uk

Collins is a registered trademark
of HarperCollins Publishers Ltd

10 09   08   07   06   05   04
7   6   5   4   3   2

© Talkback Productions Ltd 2004
Photography © Tyson Sadlo 2004

Photography: Tyson Sadlo
Photographic Production: Nicola Pedlingham

Art Direction: Mark Thomson
Editor: Pippa Rubinstein

A catalogue record for this book is available
from the British Library

ISBN 0-00-718015-2

Colour reproduction by Saxon Photolitho, Norfolk
Printed and bound by Butler and Tanner Ltd

Collins

Contents

Foreword

Television and books have the same effect on time; they have the ability to compress it into a few yards of videotape or a few sheets of paper. Looking over the proofs for this book, as they are about to go to the printers, I'm struck by how projects which have taken years to come to fruition and sometimes as long to build have been telescoped into a few pages. Some of the photographs you see here are seductive images of beautiful places, captured moments, a split second of a process that has taken months and months to get to a half-decent stage where it might look only vaguely interesting if photographed. Other images in this book are far grittier and more than hint at the sometimes gruelling experience of building a house abroad.

And *Grand Designs* is about both: the process and the beauty shots, the slow and physically hard job of building a dwelling by hand, day after day, and the finished result. *Grand Designs* is also about the vision behind all the work that drives the project, the big picture, the dream that people have and how that dream is built and embodied within the bricks and mortar of the homes that come to be.

A year and a half has passed since we started to film the experiences of the people whose work and whose houses appear here. That's a big chunk of time: a long time to be building (and filming for that matter, thank you very much), and a big slice out of the lives of these people who have all put their world on hold while they embark on a madcap adventure to start again in a foreign country.

I say that these projects are a big slice out of peoples'

lives – of course, they are nearly always the opposite: a positive and enriching experience. Putting your world on hold often means exchanging it for another undiscovered world. To design and build your own home is to go on an adventure. Because of our primitive attachments to our nests, throwing them to the wind and looking around to start again is akin in scale to selling up and trying to sail around the world or trek to the North Pole. That may sound exaggerated, but the emotional and physical demands made on people going through the big change of building a bespoke house are comparable. That's because they've uprooted themselves in a similar way and are embracing change in a big way. As a result they often become different people: enriched, wiser and, er, much, much more tired.

And if building in the UK is fraught and exhausting, it can seem like a morning at Legoland compared to what can go wrong abroad. Cultural differences, problems of language and translation, local customs, labyrinthine planning laws, town hall bureaucracy, termites, building fines, arcane historic bodies, different building materials, unusual tools, month-long national holidays, siestas, nationalized utilities, regional taxes, VAT, water shortages, blistering heat, freezing cold, mosquitoes, lack of Marmite and just downright anti-British xenophobia have got in the way of our heroic builders. I'm surprised any of them stuck it out so long. I'm surprised some of them even started.

In the following pages, we cover a lot of what can go wrong and look, in particular, at the detailed processes of purchasing and getting planning approval in Europe. I'm often asked why we don't cover these initial stages more thoroughly in the films, and the answer is that it's because we actively look for projects that are through the early phase and ready to go: that way we know (well, hope) we're going to see a finished house. Because the programme structure revolves around the physical process that we see, it's very hard to take the narrative back in time. This is an editorial, television thing and not a book thing, and so we've been able to include these thornier early-stage issues in this volume: for once, it's been a pleasure to be able to write about things like retrospective planning permission and the niceties of lawyers' contracts. In fact, it's been positively

interesting to pursue the many differences between other countries' and the UK's practices, perhaps chief of which is the enlarged role that an architect plays abroad. Generally speaking, in European countries your architect will be responsible for much more than his British equivalent: for ensuring that your design meets building regulations; that it's engineered safely and complies with any permissions and restrictions. He may even be responsible for bringing the project in on time and budget. We'll have a few more like that over here, please.

Of course, what you won't read about here or see on the box are those stories of the people who didn't stick it out, stories of the people we began filming who started a project only for it to founder immediately or for it to move so imperceptibly slowly it might as well have foundered. There are no names to be given here, not because there is any shame attached to failing in such harsh adversity. Rather, there is great honour: these are the unnamed fallen, the soldiers for whom greatness lies in having sacrificed their project to the greater glory of self-builders across Europe, who are the lucky few for whom victory is sweet.

Those that do give up and go home usually do so for one reason: their inability to bend and respond to what it is that drew them there in the first place. It is the insistence on being British and living British lives in another country that makes life difficult rather than easier, integration almost impossible and the understanding of local custom and practice confused. It may sound flippant, but even an unreasonable attachment to the quirkiest of British habits and day-to-day things, like working through the siesta or wearing Turnbull and Asser shirts are pretty sure-fire indicators that things are going to go *forma di pera*. I even thought we should make a separate series about these people, called 'Mad Dogs and Englishmen'.

And not speaking a language (or more bizarrely, the refusal to try) clearly doesn't help. In fact, language is fundamental, the key that unlocks your understanding of a foreign culture. Once you appreciate the diversity, quirkiness and richness of a vocabulary and foreign turns of phrase, you begin to appreciate how diverse and fully-formed the culture might be. In fact, in the case of Italian for example, you quickly come to see how much more fully formed the culture (art, music, form, beauty, good food all thought of as fundamental necessities of life) is, compared to our own. I've been struck in the last eighteen months by how those people who are really enjoying themselves abroad are those who have used language – rather than 'contacts' – as a way into the culture. They've also found an intellectual satisfaction in being able to communicate exactly what they want and explore this new world: to ask the baker, for example, the difference between the seven different types of baguette, or the ironmongers why (perhaps more usefully in their case) Makita don't sell replaceable clutchless chucks for their 520 Turbodrill in Southern Spain.

No, our Grand Designers (if we're going to call them that) are not people who rely on weekly supplies of *The Times* and HP sauce; they are not just there for the climate; they're certainly not part of a tightly-knit, ex-pat community who are there for the golf. They're people who want to embrace foreign culture, live the life, eat the food, and speak the language (all especially true if moving to the west coast of Ireland). Grand Designers are people who are anything but complacent; come to think of it, I don't think any of them in this book even play golf.

By nature of them finishing (or almost) their builds, being filmed in the process and appearing in this book, all our Grand Designers are, of course, heroes. They have trodden a path which is a hard one to follow in the UK, let alone abroad. Their stories are worth reading because they are personal adventures into new territory and of course a new life, living in a strange land. And the photographs of their houses aren't just another set of interiors shots taken for a magazine. They are a record of that adventure.

Introduction

When the poets Byron and Shelley lived in Italy during the early nineteenth century, they were exiles not only because of a whole host of personal reasons, but also in large part due to the degree of difficulty that they faced in returning home – a journey that would take weeks and involve considerable risks.

Perhaps if the two of them had been able to return via cheap flights from Venice or Bologna, they might well have done. However, it is hard to conjure with the image of Byron sitting on a budget aeroplane and decanting four or five mini-bottles of red wine into the skull from which he regularly used to imbibe.

Things have not only got a lot easier in terms of long-distance transport and communications in the last 200 years, but, more significantly, they have improved spectacularly in the last ten years. It means that you can now fly around Europe relatively inexpensively and, if you choose to live abroad, it is far easier to keep in touch with friends and family via e-mail and mobile telephones. It also means that you can stay tuned to what is happening in your home country via the Internet or satellite television, enjoying an engagement with a new cultural milieu without being entirely alienated from your own. Of course, for some people this defeats the object of leaving Britain in the first place – a move motivated by a yearning for discovery, perhaps, or even disenfranchisement and disillusionment – with the weather of their native country if nothing else!

But living abroad is a major step and one potentially fraught with risk – even if you are only buying with a view to building a second home. To overcome that risk, it is best to be prepared. This means doing a lot of things – research and planning, getting legal and financial advice, checking the credentials of people who are working for you, and so on. But the first major thing you have to do is to ask yourself whether this is really what you want. And this involves looking head-on at the concrete realities that such a venture will entail.

Taking the leap

For many people, building their own house is the physical realization of a long-standing dream. But for those who choose to do it abroad, this dream is often two-fold, combining the desire to live in a bespoke home of their own with that of wanting to be in a particular place that offers something rather more intangible.

And in the age in which we live, an age of increasingly mobile societies, national boundaries represent little barrier to the fulfilment of such dreams. So in that sense there's nothing stopping you – or anyone else – from doing it as well.

The attractions seem clear. Britain is a very densely developed and populated place in contrast to many countries in Europe – such as France – and building abroad offers much more opportunity to find space and genuine rural tranquillity. In addition, land and property prices are cheaper in many parts of Europe than they are in Britain. But building abroad also offers a much greater diversity of physical landscape, from the arid plains of Spain to the spectacular mountains of the Alps – a substantial menu from which to choose for those in pursuit of natural beauty. And then there's the weather. It's the eternal bugbear of all who endure the British climate – not just the rain and long, cold winters, but the sheer unpredictability of it – the one quality that makes it so ubiquitous a topic of conversation here. A move to southern Italy or Spain, for example, means shorter winters, dependably hot summers and generally far more predictable patterns of weather. And that climate gives you the chance to pursue the type of lifestyle that is so desirable to so many people, and which in the main is fairly inaccessible in Britain. It's the lifestyle of al fresco dining – not just in the midday heat, but well into the evening and night; the promise of long, languid days around a swimming pool or in the shade of a vine; the lure of a warm sea or the delicious cool of mountain rivers. 'A change in the weather is sufficient to create the world and ourselves anew,' remarked Proust. And the sense of renewal would also seem to be a significant one for anybody contemplating building a house abroad – not only because of the different climate, but because of the full breadth of different experience that it offers. There is the chance of a new start in a wide variety of ways: a new culture to explore, new places to visit, new forms of recreation to pursue and a new language to learn.

Of course, this is assuming you go the whole hog and make your new house your permanent home, rather than a second or holiday home. The difference between the two is rather like the difference between scuba diving and snorkelling. With scuba diving you are fully immersed; with snorkelling you generally remain on the surface, only making occasional forays into the depths. There are advantages and disadvantages to both, dependent as much on your attitude to life as anything else. Naturally, expense is also a key consideration: if we could all afford holiday homes, their incidence would be far more widespread. But the long-term considerations are worth thinking about if you are going to make your permanent home abroad. Then you face the possible risk of feeling estranged from friends and family in Britain and being alienated by a foreign language, culture and bureaucratic conventions, leaving you potentially isolated and unhappy. This totally undermines the whole concept of trying to improve the quality of life that you had in the first place. If you have enough money to keep a home in Britain, though, you may never reap the rich rewards that are on offer from learning and engaging fully with a new culture and integrating with a new community. But a second home could also deliver financial rewards if you are prepared to lease it to other people.

However, whether you are doing a new build or a major restoration, it will probably take many months and you will have to engage extensively with local people and learn how local procedures (planning and construction, for example) work anyway – unless, perhaps, you are wealthy enough to get someone to do all this for you! So whatever the ultimate fate of your home, you'll have to take a deep breath and dive right into it at the outset; if you don't have the will or desire to do that, it's probably best not to start. Having some knowledge of the language and an appetite to learn are fairly essential prerequisites. You'll also need a healthy dose of mental strength, endurance, courage, willpower and common sense, while a positive attitude to research and planning will definitely be useful.

Taking a leap like this isn't something you do lightly. You've got to evaluate whether a home abroad is going to bring you the benefits you want in life, and at what cost those benefits will be delivered.

Through telling the stories of eight sets of people who've undertaken this massive adventure themselves, we hope to provide an insight into some of the potential benefits and downfalls this experience can bring – and how much it can cost.

However, it is ultimately up to you whether you want to take the plunge and actually go for it, a decision that, for most people at least, will be based upon some pretty extensive thought and research. That's the safest approach to it, anyway. But there are people who prefer to do things impulsively, take risks and live dangerously; without such people many buildings would never get built. We've tried to provide practical, sensible advice in this book, but realize that where dreams and adventure are concerned, this will only go so far.

But it's a good idea, at the very least, to ask as

many questions as possible throughout the process – and to try to get decent answers to most of them. Perhaps the first two vital things to ask are questions for yourself: where you are going to build and what are you going to build there? 'Where' will probably be a decision based on a fairly complex set of factors – and it is a good idea to develop as broad a set of criteria, as possible. You have to think about financial aspects, such as how much property or land would cost; how much regular visits to the site from the UK will be, and, if you are intending to stay near the build, what rental prices are like. Depending on the type of build you're considering, you may want to choose an area that has a particular planning culture you feel would be preferential to you. You might also want to find somewhere that provides all the facilities, amenities and natural beauty that you would expect from your ideal location.

The second consideration is whether you're going to renovate or build a new house from scratch. If you have a general love of old buildings, or a particular fantasy home that involves one – perhaps a Genoese watchtower in Corsica, or a castle in Tuscany – then restoration would seem to be for you. Similarly, if you have a love of modern design or see the project as an opportunity to realize a unique example of architecture, then a new build would seem to be the preferred choice. That's all fairly obvious.

But if you think that restoration is going to be the less expensive option, think again.

It's possibly tempting when you see a rickety old French farmhouse on the market for £20,000 to think that it's a bargain that can be tarted up quite nicely for not too vast a sum of money. But ruins will generally cost a lot more to restore than you might think, and they can turn into bottomless pits that seem to eat up your cash. Make sure you get an estimate before you buy. And if you are thinking about a new build, beware of planning laws in certain places – parts of Italy, for example – where building is made prohibitively expensive unless you own an enormous area of land. These things are not necessarily complicated; they just require a certain amount of research.

In addition, a whole array of other considerations need to be taken into account, such as checking residency requirements, taxes and the issue of financing the project. In particular, you need to ask yourself the fundamental question, 'Can I afford it?' In a project with as many potential complexities as this, that calculation will require close scrutiny of a number of different elements on top of the costs associated with the purchase of land and the construction.

Turning a rubble-strewn hillside into a majestic Italian castle takes a lot of time and plenty of money... but the rewards are clear to see.

Can you afford it?

There is obviously a plethora of considerations to take into account when embarking on a project as complex as building a house abroad, but it's probably the financial factors that have to be thought about in most depth first of all.

Of course, being able to afford something often depends on what you take the word 'afford' to mean. For some it means not having to borrow any money at all in order to accomplish their goal. For others – perhaps most – affordability relates to a complicated formula of savings, borrowing, equity and future income. The most extreme example of interpretation is among people who may have anxieties about being mortgaged up to the hilt, but who are sure as hell not going to let it stop them from building their dream home. The borrowing culture in which we live encourages us to pursue our aspirations as we usually need financial help in realizing them, but it is up to you to determine how much risk you are really willing to take on.

Building your own home abroad is not something you are going to be able to do if you have very little spare cash lying around, and it would be unrealistic to portray it as a dream accessible to all. But it's also not just the preserve of the ultra-wealthy, and in many cases building abroad is ultimately less expensive than it is in Britain. Indeed, that may be one of the prime motivating forces in doing it in the first place. For example, of the eight projects featured in this book, the cheapest plot was bought for a mere £15,000, and quite a few others for less than £50,000, including 8 acres in Spain with a cottage already on it for just £45,000. However, you need to take considerable care that you don't leap in to buy cheap land or a ruin that seems incredibly good value without first doing some more stringent calculations about the long-term wisdom of that move. This particularly applies to renovations, which can often turn into financial quagmires if you're not careful to make detailed checks at the outset.

Budgeting for your build has to take into account a variety of costs. Let's look at a few of these. First, from the very beginning of the process, it's a good idea to employ a lawyer who is an expert in property law in the country in which you're buying. Regardless of whether you're in France or Italy, Spain or Ireland, purchasing property has certain pitfalls, and using a lawyer should help protect your interests and make sure key details, such as the status of deposits, are clarified. He or she will also be able to draw up contracts with key contractors. But lawyers, as we all know, are expensive, and their fees need to be factored into your total budget.

Then there is the cost of the land or property itself and any taxes associated with its purchase. However, before you buy the land it is an extremely good idea to have an understanding of what you will be able to gain approval for on the site. If you're not going to be able to get planning permission for what you want to do, then it's a good idea to establish this fact before you buy and save yourself some money from the outset! It's also a good idea to remember that there are statutory charges for obtaining planning permission in most countries – an additional cost to factor in.

You will almost certainly be employing an architect to draw up plans for you and submit information for planning applications, as in most countries this is mandatory for all but the smallest of buildings. This is another significant cost to calculate into your sums. How significant will depend on whether you want the architect to play a continuing role as a project architect, or whether the initial design and planning stages will be the full extent of his or her involvement. You may also wish to use more than one architect: one (perhaps British-based) for devising the initial design and plans for example, and a second, local architect for submission of planning information and project work. Three sets of people in

this book – in Malaga, Alicante and Les Gets – have done precisely that. It's also possible that you will have to employ other professionals in addition to your architect – a structural engineer, a quantity surveyor and a project manager, for example.

And then there's the cost of the building itself. You need to have a sensible figure that has been worked out well in advance of starting the build in order for you to assess whether it's realistic for you to begin. An estimate might be provided by your project architect, if you're using one, though this will almost certainly be a fairly rough figure. Nonetheless, it will also be a useful one to compare contractors' quotes against. You might instead decide to consult a quantity surveyor. If you are purchasing from a single contractor, who will be employing a number of subcontractors, it makes your sums rather easier, though not necessarily smaller! You may instead be directly employing a stonemason, carpenter, roofer, electrician and plumber, and have to obtain individual quotes from each. Alternatively, if you are intending to do the construction work and source the materials yourself, then it is your responsibility to come up with a realistic quote that takes all details into consideration – including a comprehensive site insurance policy.

Another significant cost that you have to factor in is that of essential services – mainly electricity, water and sewerage. Are you going to be able to connect your property easily to these utilities, or will you have to find alternative solutions, such as solar or geothermal energy, water wells or rain collection, or a septic tank? Whatever solution is appropriate for you is likely to involve an extra cost, though with renewable energy, for example, you will end up saving money after an initial capital investment.

Bespoke buildings almost never come in below budget, so it's good to be aware of that fact while you are in the formative stages of preparing your own figures. This is mainly a result of the fact that they are unique buildings – prototypes – and, as such, do not have dependable time-frames and costs for construction. Unforeseen problems often occur, and new design decisions have to be made. So there's a major element of risk here that even the most careful of planning can never entirely remove.

But good planning is essential if you want to try to keep costs down. In part, this is about providing specifications in as much detail as possible and leaving nothing to the imagination. If you take into account the price of fixtures and fittings, landscaping, insulation and finishes at the beginning, you won't get into the mentality later on of saying, 'Well, we've already spent £200,000 on the house, so what's another £25,000 on a super-chic bathroom going to matter?'

Planning is also essential in terms of timing: in crude terms, the quicker the house is built, the less it is going to cost. Of course, that doesn't mean you should compromise on quality. But you should do everything within your power to keep delays to a minimum and get the construction side of the project completed as quickly as possible.

If initial estimates seem exorbitantly high, there are still opportunities to reduce the cost of the build before you begin. Making sure you have got the lowest quotes possible from reputable contractors is a good start. You may also decide that certain details or specifications of the building can be sacrificed, or, indeed, the whole scale of the building reduced in order to bring the cost down. Another alternative, viable only if you have enough space, is to do the interior fit only on the sections of the house that are absolutely essential for living in. You can then raise additional funds to complete the remaining work at a later date. And instead of having an army of workers on site the whole time, you could do a lot of the work yourself, as many people in *Grand Designs Abroad* have done.

A lot of costs are not going to be incurred on the site itself, though, but in getting to and from it. These sums are dependent upon whether you're going to be moving to a location near the site – or even on it – or whether you'll be remaining in Britain and visiting the site sporadically. This in turn will mostly be influenced by whether this is going to be your main home or a second home. But the fact that the build will probably be easily accessible only by air travel indicates that this cost area is likely to be relatively high. Even if you are on a route served by a budget operator, there are significant other costs, such as car hire and accommodation. And once you have started the build, the desire, and perhaps the need, to see it and supervise what is happening on a regular basis means that you'll be making a large number of trips.

If you decide to base yourself near the build, the cost of accommodation may also be a significant one, dependent on how long the build takes. But staying in a caravan on site through the winter is perhaps a more practical measure of cost-saving in, say, southern Italy than it would be in Northumbria!

Planning, care and attention to detail will help in calculating financial matters, but you should be prepared for the unexpected. Building abroad is not for the faint-hearted, and a large amount of grit, determination and enterprise will be almost as useful as an extra few thousand euros! If you have a realistic budget and some form of contingency fund, though, you have a steady foundation for the transformation of your home from a collection of plans into the tangible realization of your dreams.

Reflecting on a job well done is a stage you are only likely to reach after a great deal of planning and a lot of hard work.

What do you want?

Mick Jagger may have been right when he said, 'You can't always get what you want,' but building abroad is one instance where you should do your level best to prove him wrong and get exactly what you want.

Indeed, surely the greatest motivation in undertaking the project of building your own home is being able to get from it what you're after – not only in terms of the design and specification of the house but also in terms of its exact location. You've got to think about what both house and location have to do for you and your partner or family, and what are your essential 'must-haves' for the property.

Probably the best, and certainly the most organized, way to do this is to work out a detailed set of briefs to cover both the location and the design. A brief is simply a list of criteria that you want satisfied. So you might begin by specifying a general brief for the area in which you want to build, which takes into account both practical aspects and the less tangible things that are especially inspirational to you.

area brief
|| Near the sea (i.e. within a 20-minute car journey)
|| Within a one- or two-hour drive of an airport serviced by budget flights to and from the UK
|| Not more than an hour away from a major town with good shopping facilities, areas of significant cultural interest, etc.
|| Somewhere that's exceptionally beautiful
|| An area with affordable land/property prices
|| An area with a clearly understandable and reasonable planning culture

Of course, this is only an example. But it illustrates how you can start to make some headway into what can seem an enormous task at the outset. However, it's possible that from the very beginning your dream had only one particular area in mind, perhaps somewhere that you had fallen in love with on a holiday or succession of holidays. If this is the case, it's important to check whether the practical aspects of living there will match the sublime nature of your surroundings.

The only way to really get to know an area and gain an understanding of whether it's the right place for you is to visit it as often as you can during different times of the year: it's likely to look markedly different in December and July, for instance. If you're looking to build a second home that you might also want to lease out, then you should probably evaluate how attractive it is as a destination for tourists throughout the year. But whether or not it's a permanent or second home, you will benefit from trying to find out as much as possible about the area: talk to local people; visit the local town hall and find out about the process of obtaining planning permission; read as much as you can. It's also worth trying to find out about any major future developments in the region, such as road building, which could be either a benefit or a blight from your point of view. And be aware that budget air services, which are often routed to smaller airports, are liable to change, or may even be withdrawn entirely, meaning that it's probably best not to rely too heavily on this particular benefit to the exclusion of others.

Once you have found a general region that you would like to build in, you then need to find a specific site. Admittedly, it may not work quite as neatly as this, and you may find a plot or renovation project before you have had a chance to research the area. But in looking for either, it's a good idea, once again, to prepare a brief that could be given to an estate agent, for example.

brief for a new build

|| The size of plot
|| On a hillside or not – with a particular type of view (sea, mountains, sunset, etc.)
|| If it is on a hillside, what direction the hillside should face
|| Soil type
|| The type of access there is to the plot
|| Proximity to a (particular) town, village or other facilities
|| Ability to connect easily to utilities
|| Immediate surroundings (isolated or on the periphery of a town, etc.)
|| Cost

brief for a renovation

In addition to the relevant points above, you would also need to specify:
|| The type and age of building you're after (castle, farmhouse, church, etc.)
|| The size of the building and plot
|| The structural condition of the building

There may be other aspects that you would like to specify as well. But even if your brief is very explicit, it's still likely that estate agents will drag you off to see a number of places that fit very few – or even none – of your criteria. However, having this prescriptive list should tighten up your search enormously and, with luck, enable you to find the site that you really want. Even if it does fit all the points you have specified, though, it will also need to have some indefinable quality – something that gives you an intuitive feeling that it's right.

And once you have found your site or property, the real excitement of working out what you want to do with it begins. Having a very strong idea from the start about precisely what you would like the end-product to look like may be part of the whole process of making your dreams real, but you also need to have a degree of flexibility and the ability to think about how the ideas in your head are going to translate to the particular site on which you are building. It's especially pertinent to think about how, in the case of a new build, your house will fit into the natural landscape and built environment that surrounds it. A renovation project, on the other hand, requires you to think about the character of the building that you are bringing back to life.

To a large extent these contextual realities will be dictated to you by the planning authority that's going to approve – or refuse – your plans. It's a good idea to have a reasonable understanding of what you're going to be able to build before you buy the land. And there is no way that a large, erotic gherkin is ever going to get permission among the sunflowers and vines of Tuscany, or a glass and concrete box among the wooden chalets of the Alps! Remember, though, it's not just your building that has to integrate into its environment – you do as well. And the building itself can become an apt metaphor for your own efforts at fitting in. So when you're thinking about design decisions you might want to bear in mind that getting on with the neighbours could be important. This might seem doubly so when you understand that planning permission in many countries in mainland Europe does not so much rely on statute as a localized consensus-based politics. This means that being on good terms with local people is going to aid the process, while alienating them could do great harm.

With these considerations in mind, you need to start the process of getting a formal design drawn up. In order for the end-product to be in sympathy with your vision, it's best to prepare a brief for whoever is designing your building, in most cases an architect. This is your opportunity to impress upon the architect what you consider to be the fundamental criteria that the building will have to satisfy. These should be both aesthetic and practical and take into account your lifestyle. These choices are obviously going to be dependent on your tastes, but this architect's brief includes some of the things to consider:

architect's brief

|| The number and types of rooms

|| The size of certain rooms

|| The orientation of the building (e.g. the front is south-facing)

|| The overall 'philosophy' of the building (e.g. simple, environmentally friendly dwelling that blends well into the landscape, or a modernist cube, or a holiday home traditional for the area, etc.)

|| The relationship between your building and surrounding buildings

|| The specification of certain areas for certain activities (e.g. veranda for sitting in shade and reading a book in the heat of the midday sun)

|| The primary materials that you would like to be used (inside and out)

|| Essential specifications of rooms (e.g. living room or kitchen 'must-haves')

|| Type and extent of heating/ventilation

|| Views; will windows require shutters?

|| Lighting

|| Environmental criteria (e.g. levels of insulation, solar power, energy-efficient heating, water recycling, water collection, levels of passive solar gain)

|| Other major features (e.g. swimming pool, garden)

Ultimately, the brief is going to include everything you consider to be essential, and in drawing it up you shouldn't hold back: go for what you really want. It will help the architect enormously and ultimately create a design that is unique.

In deciding what materials should be used – particularly the main construction materials – it is worth looking at what is going to be easily obtainable in the area in which you're building, and what local workers are going to be most adept at using. Unless you intend importing a workforce or doing the construction yourself, you'll probably need a number of skilled local workers on site. And in most localities there will be a particular specialization – Spanish builders, for example, will, in the main, be used to working with steel and concrete. This is a further reason behind conformity of building style in certain regions – local tradesmen are only really used to working in a particular way. This in turn may dissuade you from trying to construct a building in materials that will be unfamiliar to local tradesmen, as perhaps they won't be able to provide the expertise you need to achieve a good result.

The types of materials you use may also be influenced by environmental factors. The environment continues to suffer from mankind's devastating and brutal engagement with it, and house-building is an indubitably harmful activity. This is true not only because of the methods and materials employed in the actual construction process, but because we continue to manufacture ecologically destructive buildings that have enormous energy needs for fundamental requirements, such as heating, ventilation and lighting. Here you can make a difference. You could start by thinking about what is called the 'embodied energy' of the individual materials you're using, that is, the amount of energy and consequent carbon dioxide emissions that have gone into manufacturing them and transporting them to the site. Wood and stone, for example, will have very low embodied energy levels – particularly if they are locally sourced – while steel and glass will be very high. You should not only think about the embodied energy of certain materials, though, but of the cumulative energy that you spend getting to and from the site. As supervising the project will probably involve a relatively large amount of air travel, this is likely to represent a big chunk of your building's total embodied energy. There are a few things you can do to try and 'pay back' this energy. Using recycled materials is one method, and if you're renovating a building, you are, of course, already recycling on a massive scale. But it's also possible to use reclaimed wood and bricks, or waste materials, such as straw bales. And you could also plant trees on your site in order to offset carbon dioxide emissions. Trees absorb carbon dioxide and pump oxygen back into the air – but you'll need to plant a small forest to offset a lot of air travel.

The other two major forms of decreasing overall energy impact are by procuring your energy from clean sources and using materials effectively to ensure that the building is energy efficient. Building in a dependably sunny climate means that solar panels are an exceptionally good means of providing clean energy. If you're building in such a climate, the main challenge is likely to be ventilating and cooling the building effectively. But cooler conditions create an opposite challenge – heat retention. In this case, techniques such as using large, south-facing windows to maximize passive solar gain, and materials that provide 'thermal mass' – effectively soaking up and retaining the heat – provide an environmentally friendly solution to keeping your house warm.

You may also want to consider the toxicity of certain materials, which are not only harmful to the environment but potentially directly harmful to you. It's a good idea to check all highly processed materials for their levels of toxicity.

Ending up with a location, site and design that you are happy with may depend upon a number of other people, but your own role should not be under-estimated. Good communication in the form of clear and detailed briefs will help other people to understand your aims and objectives, making it easier for them to find a site, or conceive a design, that offers exactly what you want.

However, your building still remains largely in the realm of the theoretical – it's a drawing or model, rather than the palpable dream you would love it to be. So you now need to decide who is going to be responsible for implementing the design in order not only to have your cake, but eat it as well!

Your team

In simple terms, there are three main elements to a build – the design, the project management and the construction itself. These apparently discrete roles naturally seem to suggest the use of three primary players – an architect, a project manager and a main contractor.

But the choice is actually far more complex, and can depend on a number of different factors, including your budget, how much you personally want to get involved and any previous experience you might have in the building business. Let's look at each of the elements of the build in turn to see what choices you face in assembling the team who will ultimately deliver your dream home.

Design

You might decide that you don't want an architect to design your home. It's your dream and you're the one who's going to turn it into reality. An architect will only corrupt the purity of your ideas and bend them to suit his or her own conceptual whims and desires. Then there's the fact that architects are expensive: doing it yourself would save so much money.

But architects also have a great deal of formal training and experience that they can use to translate your dreams and ideas into a more formal design. To make sure there is no confusion and that you get the design you want from the architect, it's a good idea to prepare a comprehensive brief as described previously. Architects should also be able to save you money as their expertise makes them aware of potential problems that can arise in builds and allows them to factor everything into the original design. They will also work a lot more quickly than someone who is doing it for the first time. And in many countries it's not a matter of choice – you have to use a registered architect to submit information for planning permission and to sign off the various stages of the build. Indeed, having a local architect familiar with planning permission procedure on hand throughout the build can also pay significant dividends, particularly if you encounter any problems or if there is a need for clarification on certain points of the plan.

Project management

As with the design, you might decide that you would like to take on the project management of the build yourself. This involves planning the build so that the correct materials and workmen are on site at the right times for the right jobs, while controlling all the costs. Sounds simple, doesn't it? And if you are able to be on site for the duration of the build, it makes things a lot easier than if you're trying to manage things from a different country. But project management can be a lot tougher than it appears, so it's worth considering some other options before you make the decision to go it alone.

You could get your architect to be your project manager, though this is probably the most expensive option available to you. The advantages are that he or she knows the design better than anyone else and is therefore probably in the best position to implement it. Alternatively, you might want to get the main contractor to do all the project management for you on your behalf. As he will be directly subcontracting most of the works on site, this is probably the most practical option.

The final option is to employ a separate project manager who is neither an architect nor a builder, but who acts as a contractor and quantity surveyor and who manages all the subcontractors brought on to site. Although this may be a realistic option in Britain, it's not generally so if you are building abroad, where this method, on the whole, is simply not used.

Construction

The person responsible for your project management will dictate, to a large extent, who you choose to be your workforce. If you are using a contractor or architect as your project manager, he will subcontract the work directly. If you are project managing yourself, then it is up to you to do this.

With all contractors it is a good idea to seek out a personal recommendation, get references, see previous work and even talk to previous clients. Get a number of quotes from different contractors before you commit to any one. You will also need to get legal help in drawing up a contract that sets out requirements and terms, and that should be signed before any work begins.

When employing your own sub-contractors, it's also important to get recommendations, references and see examples of recent work that they have undertaken.

The final option is to do it all yourself – and some people do. But if you have never done it before, you have to learn on the job, which at best can be slow, and at worst downright dangerous (with roofing and electrics, for example). And any savings you make should be set against the fact that you will be spending a lot longer doing the build than if you employed professionals to do it for you.

Whatever team you choose to assemble, you are now in a position to begin work. It's time to watch the building of your dreams take shape – just be aware that the unexpected could be right around the corner!

Spain

Spain, in its cities at least, has a tremendous buzz and vibrancy about it right now. Its economy has been booming in recent years and it has benefited enormously from EU schemes such as road-building grants and agricultural subsidies. But Spain has also had a tumultuous history that encompasses conquest by Rome, invasion by Visigoths and 700 years of Islamic rule.

It's hard now to credit that General Franco, the last of Europe's notorious twentieth-century dictators, died only 30 years ago. And it was only in 1981 that a military coup sought to overthrow the newly established democratic system. We forget what a youthful democracy Spain is. In large part that's because for many years it has been such a popular destination, both for British holiday makers and people looking for a new or second home. Its popularity continues and, as a result, prices of land and houses are increasing, while Spain's reputation for being a cheap place to live is also being eroded as the wealth of its inhabitants increases.

The attraction nonetheless remains, due in part to the recent deluge of cheap flights to Spain. The country has an incredible diversity of landscape and two coastlines, retaining more than enough unspoilt areas to counteract the reputation of some of the places more heavily developed by tourism. In the main it has a mild climate, beautiful, cultural cities, such as Seville, Barcelona and Madrid, and wonderful food and wines.

The two builds that we will be looking at in Malaga and Alicante are both on the Mediterranean coast – and close to airports with budget flights to the UK. However, both families have eschewed the more popular tourist areas to find rather more isolated situations in which to build their vastly contrasting houses.

Andalusia (Malaga Build)

The physical variety of Andalusia in southern Spain is amazing, ranging from searingly hot desert to snow-capped mountains, and not forgetting the infamous Costa del Sol. Among the highlights of the region are the cities of Granada, Seville and Cordoba, which contain some of the most impressive monuments to the country's Moorish occupation. There are also many whitewashed towns called *pueblos blancos*. Andalusia is justly acclaimed for its food, which has been heavily influenced by Moorish cuisine and includes almonds, citrus fruits and saffron – ingredients you would just as easily find in Morocco as Spain.

Alicante (La Pedrera Build)

The stretch of coastline between Denia and Torrevieja in the south-east corner of Spain is known as the Costa Blanca, and is probably the area most familiar to British visitors. The whole area has been a development hotspot, but Torrevieja has been one of the fastest-growing urban zones in Europe in the last ten years. It is, however, easy to escape from the built-up sprawl of places such as Alicante, the regional capital, and Benidorm, an example of development at its worst. Inland from the coastal resorts are vast citrus groves either intensely fragrant with blossom or bursting with fruit. Much of the surrounding, non-irrigated land, though, is arid scrub.

Spain: Practicalities

Buying property in Spain has long been a popular pastime for Britons, though in the main this has meant holiday apartments and villas in tourist areas such as the Costa Blanca and Costa del Sol.

However, that popularity does not necessarily translate into a purchase process and planning culture which closely resembles what happens in Britain: you might readily be able to swap fish and chips for *tapas*, but swapping planning permission for a *permiso de obra* is not quite so easy. If you're going to build or renovate in Spain, you will have to become familiar with its procedures. This also applies to the language. There are, of course, many Spaniards who speak excellent English and in the major tourist areas it is part of daily life, but there is no substitute for making the effort to talk and understand Spanish. It generates goodwill – it's as simple as that.

It's also a good idea to banish some of the pernicious stereotypes and rumours that abound about Spain. Let's examine a couple of them. First, there is a common idea that Spaniards are lazy and that daily life is dominated by a social convention called *mañana* (tomorrow). Forget it. In the last few years Spain has become one of the fastest-growing economies in the EU. Vibrant, buoyant economies are not sustained by lazy people. It is true that life has a different, and most would say a very civilized, rhythm, but it is up to incomers to adapt to that, not vice versa.

There is also the peculiar idea that Spanish builders do not work to a high standard. This is also nonsense: just as in Britain there are good builders and there are cowboys. The important thing in Spain, as in Britain, is to get references and see examples of previous work before you sign any contract with a builder.

Note that the Spanish town hall (*ayuntamiento*) has far more power than in Britain. In practical terms this makes it advisable to be on good terms with a few key people; introducing yourself to the town clerk and discussing your plans is always a good start.

The purchase process

You've got to think about exactly what you want to get out of where you are living in Spain. There is plenty of variety in terms of physical landscape, and consequently of climate too. Mainland Spain has Europe's only desert, a number of major mountain ranges including the Pyrenees and the Sierra Nevada, and a Mediterranean and Atlantic coastline. And there are also the Canary and Balearic Islands that you may wish to consider. Always try to find out as much as you can about the location that you are thinking about: facilities, proximity to airports, culture, food and climate are some specific things you may want to research. Visit it as often as you can before you buy and at different times of the year: it may look very different in autumn or winter from spring or summer.

Selecting the property and researching it

Whether you are thinking about a new build or a renovation may influence the method that you use to find your property. If you are looking for a building to restore there are many websites that specialize in Spanish property, though it is likely that you will have to trawl through websites rammed full of villas and apartments on the costas in order to find a crumbling wreck that needs salvaging. However, there are numerous properties – mainly *fincas rusticas* (rural cottages) – that are available to purchase. You may also wish to look in magazines and broadsheet newspaper supplements. Magazines that specialize in Spanish property include *Spanish Homes* and *Spanish Property Directory*.

However, probably the best option – almost certainly if you are looking for land – is to give a brief to one or more local estate agent or agents (*agencias inmobiliarias*) in the area or areas in which you are looking. Estate agents should belong to a professional body called the *Agentede Propiedad Inmobiliari* (*API*). Giving them a brief means – theoretically at least – that you can cut out all the chaff that you're not going to be even vaguely interested in. Of course, what commonly happens is that agents will take you to properties and land that they're having difficulty in selling as well as those that fit your criteria! Agents' fees are usually very high in Spain with the average commission rate being approximately 10 per cent – something that you should fix with an agent before you view any properties.

USEFUL INTERNET SITES

www.andaluciandreamhomes.com
www.easypropertyspain.co.uk
www.newspanishproperty.com
www.uk2spainonline.com
www.4avilla.com

There are many anecdotes about disreputable and bogus agents in Spain ripping off British punters in pursuit of their dreams in the sun. These horror stories often cast other Brits as the villains but whether your agent happens to be British or Spanish, you should take the following precautions in order to safeguard your interests:

|| **Use a Spanish lawyer – called an** *abogado* **– who is not associated with either the agent or buyer, to check all contracts and agreements.**
|| **Ensure that any money – a deposit for example – goes to a blocked account where no party can get at it until the sale is completed or, in certain instances, defaulted. You should not pay a cash deposit direct to the agent; the blocked account is an ideal compromise.**
|| **Make sure you are aware of what the terms of the deposit are – returnable or non-returnable – in the event of failing to complete the transaction.**
|| **Any deposit paid should be linked to a contract checked by your lawyer.**

Your lawyer is going to be a key player in the transaction, so it helps to make sure you have a good one who is both honest and reliable. He or she will be able to guide you through a number of essential procedures that include obtaining a fiscal identification number (NIE) for you, completing the conveyancing of property and giving you advice on contractual and payment matters. Some of the complexities of buying rural land in particular benefit from a lawyer's input. If your Spanish is not good, then a bilingual lawyer would obviously be preferable. If you do know people in Spain, try to get a recommendation. Many people will be recommended lawyers by their agent. This may be fine, but if you want to safeguard your interests fully, you will get a recommendation from a neutral third party.

Once you have looked at some properties and found something that you like, it is important to check what you will be allowed to do on the land, whether you are contemplating a new build or a renovation. The best way to do this is to speak directly to people in the local planning department (*urbanismo*), telling them of your intentions and getting feedback from them as to whether they feel the work would be permitted.

At this early stage you will not be getting definite answers – a formal application has to be made before approval can be officially granted – but you will get a sense of whether or not your plans are likely to receive sanction. If there are problems, you should try and discuss them at this initial phase of talks. Similarly, if there seems to be broad support for your plans, then it is a good idea to try to strengthen that approval by obtaining a letter from the town clerk or planning officer that provides assurances, in principle at least, for your development. This may not be a legally binding document, but it does provide you with a degree of confidence that your plans will ultimately gain approval. This phase should also help you to develop personal relationships with vital players in the process – something that's as valuable as any piece of paper in terms of planning (see more on planning permission overleaf).

You should also obtain a copy of the *plan parcial* – a diagram that locates the plot – from the local planning department or town hall. It shows other adjacent developments and will provide information about whether any major new public works – new roads, for example – are planned nearby. It's also a good idea to check about the ease

The bureaucracy involved in Spanish property transaction requires careful attention to detail.

of connection to utilities if you are contemplating a new build or renovating a property that has been standing derelict for many years.

'Brown envelope culture' is not prevalent in Spain, but there are commonplace tax dodges that, even though you may wish to avoid them, are necessary to participate in, since everybody does. The first of these is the two different values that are generally quoted for property and land. The declared, and lesser, value is the value of the property which will be quoted in the deed (*escritura*) on which tax must be paid; the undeclared, significantly higher value is the 'real price' exclusive of tax or fees. The declared value can be paid with a banker's draft (you will need a Spanish bank account to organize this), while the difference is generally paid to the vendor in cash as 'black money'.

The first formal stage in the buying process, once you have been quoted a price and have made enquiries about planning, is a reservation contract which should take the property or land off the market. Get this document checked over by your lawyer. It is essential that it quotes the declared value and whether or not that includes IVA (VAT) in the total. It should also include the reservation, deposit and completion details.

You should then obtain the *nota simple*, a document issued by the land registry office, which is a copy of the property registration details. It will show proof that the vendor is the registered owner of the land and that there are no debts on it. All you need to do to obtain this document is visit the local land registry office, complete a form and pay a small fee. The *nota simple* will be ready for collection within a couple of days.

Negotiations and the contract

As long as the *nota simple* document provides the answers that you hope and expect, you should then get a purchase contract (*contrato privado de compraventa*) drawn up – the most important document in this entire process. It should set out all the details of the property or land that you are buying, the total declared price, payment method and penalties in the event of defaulting. It needs to be checked by your lawyer and signed by both purchaser and vendor.

However, the process is only completed once you have visited the office of the public notary (*notario*), and signed the property deed (*escritura*). If you are unable to be present at the signing, it is possible to grant your lawyer power of attorney to attend and sign on your behalf. The vendor should also be present at this signing.

The notario is the state representative in this transaction but it's not his responsibility to make sure you are getting a fair deal. The signing of the contract effectively seals all the terms and conditions of the purchase; the notary stage merely provides the state's rubber stamp which gives you the official deed. Upon signature you will be issued with a simple, unsigned copy of the deed; the first authorized copy becomes available at a later date after further administration, while the original stays in the notary's office.

There is now one final piece of documentation in the buying process: the *registro de la propiedad*. This is the registration of the deed of your property, which means that your ownership is recognized by the local land registry.

You are finally in a position to commence with your project – all you need now is formal permission.

Starting your renovation

In all cases but the very simplest of works, you will need an architect (*arquitecto*) who is registered in Spain to draw up plans and submit them to the local planning department for approval. This is true even if you have used a British architect to come up with the design. It is best to get a personal recommendation for a local architect, and make sure that you get references and check out previous work that he or she has undertaken. The local planning department may be able to recommend someone to you. This route can have advantages, as an architect used to working with a particular planning department is likely to gain the maximum flexibility from the planning officers.

Your architect not only has responsibility for submitting plans for permission, but also for confirming that the building has been constructed to a satisfactory standard in conformance to the original drawings. He does this by supplying a *certificado final de la dirección de la obra*.

Planning permission

You should already have an indication of whether you will receive permission (*permiso de obra*) from the local planning office; this should have influenced your decision to buy. If you have bought property in an area already designated for development then you should have relatively few problems. However, rural areas are far more tightly controlled and rather than conforming to uniform national rules, they vary enormously in their strictness and the type of regulation they impose.

The general trend in Spain, though, is towards greater strictness, particularly in rural planning where there is an increasingly prevalent culture of preserving areas of outstanding natural beauty and curbing development. For this reason, structures that seek to fit in with the natural environment and the context of surrounding buildings will be favoured over those that do not.

It's up to your architect to submit the necessary plans for approval at this stage. If the case is deemed straight-forward, a decision may be made within a matter of weeks. If the decision is more complex, though, a period of consultation and compromise may ensue, often leading to permission being granted. Depending on the type of work being contemplated, the *permiso de obra* will cost up to 4 per cent of the total value of the build.

It's not at all advisable to build without permission since the consequences, unsurprisingly, can be serious. If permission has not been granted, or an alteration is in breach of local regulations, a fine of 5 per cent of the alteration value is imposed, provided that the work done

has been completed satisfactorily and can be retrospectively approved. But if a breach has taken place that cannot receive retrospective approval, a much larger fine is imposed and the building will probably have to be demolished.

Finding a builder

The rules for finding a builder are similar to those for finding an architect. The three key points are:

|| **Get a recommendation.**
|| **Get references.**
|| **See previous work.**

These simple steps should ensure that you don't end up in the hands of a bunch of cowboys. In addition, though, you should seek legal advice when drawing up a contract (*contrato*) with your builder. It is essential that their insurance details should be listed in this contract.

The other simple step for making sure everything progresses smoothly is making stage payments to the builders as construction progresses. These stages can be defined by your architect, who should also check the work at each stage and before a payment is made.

Once construction has finished and the work has been signed off by the architect, it is essential to get a *licencia de primera ocupación* (licence of first occupation), which is obtained from the town hall. This allows the property to be lived in and registers it for the purpose of paying local taxes and having services connected. Note that utility companies, particularly electricity suppliers, will not connect unregistered properties.

At last, after a fairly long and bureaucratic process, you are ready to move in!

need to know

|| Fees to estate agents are high in Spain – usually around 10 per cent – so make sure the level is agreed before you view any properties. The buyer is responsible for payment.

|| Property purchase in Spain is complex so your choice of lawyer – the *abogado* – is crucial. Use a lawyer who is not connected to either the agent or the vendor.

|| Obtain a copy of the *plan parcial*, showing plot location, from the town hall. It will show any plans for your area, including adjacent developments, as well as access to utilities.

|| Speak directly to the planning department (*urbanismo*) to get at least an informal response to the work you are planning.

|| The first stage in the process is a reservation contract which should mean the property or land is withdrawn from the market. This involves the payment of a small non-returnable deposit and gives you the opportunity to conduct checks before signing anything binding.

|| Check ownership of land or property on the *nota simple*, a copy of the property registration details issued by the Land Registry office.

|| Make sure any money, e.g. for the deposit, goes to a blocked account where no party can get at it until the sale is completed.

|| Next comes the purchase contract (*contrato privado de compraventa*), which should contain all details including the declared purchase price, payment method and penalties in case of non-completion. A full deposit is payable at this stage – usually 10 per cent. Signature of this document constitutes a binding commitment to the purchase of the property.

|| Quoting two different values for the declared and undeclared value of the property is a reasonably common tax dodge.

|| Your purchase is complete when you sign the property deed, the *escritura*, usually at the office of the public notary (*notario*) with the vendor.

Spain: context and inspiration

Spain has one of the most fascinating architectural histories in all of Europe, with an exciting mélange of building styles from different centuries, that reflect its turbulent past and eclectic tastes.

Perhaps the most significant styles are due to the Moorish occupation of much of southern Spain, which ended only in the late fifteenth century, when Granada was recaptured by the Spanish. Muslim architecture in Andalusia falls into two broad periods. First was the caliphate style brought by Arabs from the Middle East (the Mezquita in Cordoba for example). The other, later period, was that of the Maghreb style, developed by Muslims in Morocco and brought to Spain in the twelfth century. This illustrates that 'Moorish' is made up of a complex set of influences, not just one cultural persuasion. These influences have left some stunning monuments, in particular the Alhambra Palace and Generalife Gardens in Granada, the great mosque in Cordoba and the Giralda minaret in Seville – commonly cited as some of the greatest examples of Moorish architecture in the world. Even after the 'reconquest' of Spain from the Moors, however, Muslim-influenced design continued to be widely used and is known as *Mudéjar*, which is a hybrid style of Moorish and Christian elements.

The Christian dominance in northern Spain and the country as a whole from the fifteenth century onwards is clearly evidenced in a wide variety of church styles, from the Gothic cathedrals of Seville and Palma de Mallorca, to the distinctively Spanish baroque style of Churrigueresque that found its apotheosis in the sacristy of the Charterhouse of Granada. The Renaissance did not miss Spain either,

The Alhambra, Granada.

although, as with the baroque movement, it took on a highly regional idiom. This is known as plateresque, a far more ornamental and highly wrought style than is found in Italian Renaissance buildings. One of the best examples of this style is to be found at the University of Salamanca.

In more modern times the one name commonly identified with Spanish architecture is Antoni Gaudí (1852–1926), the Catalan architect who is known in particular for his spectacular, as yet unfinished, cathedral in Barcelona – the Sagrada Familia. Yet in Gaudí's creations we also see much of the vast architectural heritage of Spain. In his great cathedral there is a reminder of the Spanish Gothic tradition, while in much of his other work – such as the Güell pavilions – there are explicit references to Spain's Moorish legacy. However, Gaudí somehow transforms many of these historical influences into a fabulous phantasmagoria of infinite possibility with his mesmerizing and idiosyncratic designs.

Antoni Gaudí's benches in the Parc Güell, Barcelona.

fittings, colours and furniture, as well as the occasional more architectural reference, such as Moorish-style finials or chimney detailing.

Fincas

In terms of architecture of a less grand nature, the Spanish *finca* – often dating back to the eighteenth and early nineteenth centuries – is the vernacular building which dominates the built landscape of the countryside.

The *finca*, a one-storey rural building, is traditionally constructed from stone and render with a tiled roof, and is often positioned on a terrace set into a hillside. It has a relatively long and narrow form, with the rooms arranged in a linear fashion. This allowed for additional rooms to be built on to either end of the house. However, the roof did not provide much shade, which is surprising in such a hot climate. The normal procedure was to plant vines on frames set in front of the house to provide a cool and shady outdoor area in the summer where people could relax and eat. This had the additional function of preventing the sun from baking the walls of the house, which would be whitewashed. Its low-level form, in sympathy with the agricultural terracing of which it is such a common feature, makes it sit inconspicuously in the landscape. This is quite the opposite of the more box-shaped modern villa, which is conspicuously squat and bulky when compared to the long, slender form of the *finca*.

In the main, these modern houses are constructed differently from the *finca*, with recesses, arcades and loggias cut into them to create shade. These are also no longer made from stone and render but concrete – the predominant building material across Spain. Nonetheless, the obligatory tiled roofs and whitewashed walls remain.

The Moorish influence in Spanish design has long been absorbed into the mainstream. The finials and tiling on this house show strong traces of that influence.

OPPOSITE

Traditional *fincas* such as this one are set low into the countryside; they blend in well and use the shade of surrounding trees to keep cool in the summer.

The Moorish influence

Of the later Mahgreb style of Moorish architecture, probably the finest example is to be found in the gigantic palace-fort of Alhambra that was built in the thirteenth and fourteenth centuries under the Nasrid dynasty. It is a spectacular citadel containing the slender columns, distinctive domes and arcades of historic Moroccan buildings, as well as beautifully detailed interior decoration. The ceilings are particularly awe-inspiring, with their characteristically Islamic intricacy in such details as the stalactite and honeycomb designs.

The fact that the Moors were driven out of Spain in the fifteenth century did not eradicate all traces of their culture, and it is a legacy that continues to exert itself today in Andalusia. There are clearly still Moroccan influences in doors,

You might expect that architects would be best qualified to build a home for themselves. They're used to the design process; they know about construction and materials; their aesthetic sense is finely honed from a career in which it's relentlessly exercised. But they're also used to dealing with a client who is a third party. What is it like, then, when that third party is also the architect?

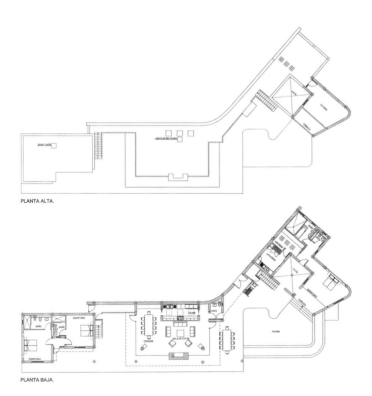

PLANTA ALTA.

PLANTA BAJA.

The plans show the tension between rectilinear shapes and the long curve of the front wall.

It could certainly lead to an element of schizophrenia, with the two roles either corresponding or clashing due to the different agendas and ideas each has. Is the client going to be generous and sympathetic or argumentative and obstreperous? And how is the architect side of the personality going to respond to this alter ego? Are they going to have a friendly relationship or raging arguments which lead to the architect walking off, arms folded, with a loud harrumph and mutterings about the client not understanding?

This latter scenario certainly does not seem to have happened with architect Gil Briffa and his wife Hilary, who manages their practice in St Albans. The couple, both in their early sixties, have built a retirement home for themselves near Malaga in southern Spain, with Gil as the project architect for the build. But 'retirement home' suggests something rather staid and boring and Gil and Hilary's house is certainly not that; it is an exciting and exemplary piece of contemporary design not only in terms of the final product but in terms of the stages that they went through to achieve it.

A very important starting point was the fact that they didn't have too many preconceptions about what the house would look like before they bought the land on which they would build it. They wanted to have a building that was designed for the specific environment in which it would sit. 'We didn't have a house in our heads that we thought: let's just find a piece of land to plonk it on,' says Gil. 'And the house we have built has evolved from that site,' adds Hilary.

So the first stage was finding the land. They started off by looking in Britain – a frustrating and ultimately futile search that lasted for two years. Gil did get excited about one plot in Devon but then deemed it too expensive to buy and develop on. And it was cost, in the main, that led

The immediate view looks over a small hamlet of white-washed houses, typical of the region.

them to look abroad. Spain was the first place that they explored abroad. This was due mainly to three fairly practical reasons – the cost of land, the climate and the fact that cheap flights to Spain went regularly from airports close to two houses that they keep in Britain: one in St Albans (Luton airport) and the other in Bath (Bristol airport).

They required certain things of the site, so when they e-mailed a number of Spanish estate agents who they had found on the Internet, they included a five-point checklist of what they wanted. The criteria were that the land had to have a total area of at least 5,000 square metres, a sea view, be connected to mains electricity and water supplies, and be easily accessible via a short track connected to a paved road. However, of the sites for which they received details, very few actually ended up fitting their specifications.

'We got flats in the centre of town, bungalows, and orange groves in the middle of nowhere,' recalls Hilary. 'Some of them were really beautiful places, but not what we were after.'

One of the estate agents was English, so, as neither Gil nor Hilary spoke Spanish, they decided to concentrate on sites recommended by him. So once he had assembled a few sites for viewing, they flew out to Malaga to reconnoitre for a week. After arriving in Spain, though, they had to wait for a few days before they saw anything, despite the agent telling them he would take them to different sites every day they were there. But on their first day's viewing they found the site that they ended up buying. And what a site it is. High up in a valley, on a south-facing slope, they were shown a wonderful patch of terraced hillside with views that look all the way down the valley towards the sea. There are

olive trees dotted all around and a number of traditional Spanish hill villages with white-walled, red-roofed houses that can be seen from the top of the plot. It is a quiet, rural place where the only sounds are of goats and cockerels, cicadas and birdsong. At the bottom of the patch of land there is a whitewashed *finca* – a traditional style Spanish cottage.

They loved it straight away. 'I can't criticize him too much,' says Gil of the estate agent, 'he came up trumps! We liked walking along the land; we liked the feel it gave us.' But before they bought the plot they wanted to make sure that they could build the home of their dreams there. If they couldn't, then it was no good. But getting assurances that planning permission would be granted wasn't an easy assignment. This was largely due to the fact that the plot they were looking at was not actually considered to be one piece of land at all, but was in fact cut up into historical divisions of land called *parcela* – literally 'a parcel'. In order to get permission for a new build you have to own a certain amount of land. However, that judgement is not made on the total area of the plot that you own, but the area of the individual parcela that you want to build on. The issue was further complicated by whether the land is classified as dry or wet: theirs was classed as dry land, meaning that you have to own much more land before you can build on it.

Gil and Hilary also wanted to build at the top of the plot – where the view is most magnificent – rather than at the bottom, where the *finca* was situated. 'Up there you are with the eagles,' says Gil. 'Down at the bottom you are with the sparrows or the finches.' But the best assurance that they could get was a written document signed by the town clerk who said they would be allowed to build another building on the lower level in the place of the existing *finca*.

During the process of negotiating this assurance, though, they met Paco, a man who would become a key player in their building, both practically and politically, because he was a political party leader at the local town hall as well as a builder. So, after Gil and Hilary had bought the land, Paco got a design and secured planning permission. He was the first person they looked to for a quote on the construction of their house.

And whatever the house would cost to build, they had found a bargain in terms of the land, particularly in the light of inflation in Spanish land prices since their purchase. For 37,500 square metres (approximately 9 acres), including the cottage and three valuable wells, they paid an

OPPOSITE
'Up with the eagles and down with the sparrows'. Gil and Hilary's new house overlooks the *finca* or cottage that was on the site when they bought it.

BELOW
The platform on which the house is set is in fact one of the terraces that start at the base of the hill. The building follows the lateral curve of the slope.

There is a vast expanse of outdoor space on the ground floor. You can see how overhangs provide shade for both interior and exterior areas.

astonishing €70,000 – about £45,000. And it was in part the evident good value of the site that led them to take the risk of buying it when they did not yet have planning permission to build what they wanted: a house on the higher level rather than lower down.

But by this time, Gil and Hilary already had preliminary drawings for the house, making the idea of compromise all the harder. These had been done for them not by Gil, but by their son, Matt, who is also an architect and a partner in the firm. The drawings were based on a detailed brief provided by his parents, setting out essential specifications and ideas that they wanted incorporated into the design. The brief is an essential part of getting an end-product that the client is going to be happy with. And this is where, as a client and an architect, Gil was able to take advantage of his knowledge and experience to ensure that he and Hilary got the result they wanted. 'We believe that clients give us very bad briefs,' he says, 'so *we* have to write them. Without it, you can't design: where do you start?'

The brief mentioned a whole variety of things; some were very specific – that the building had to be approached through a wall with only one opening in it and that some rooms were of a certain size, for example. Other ideas were less specific, such as asking that the building be well ventilated. Hilary wanted to live as much outdoors as indoors and had the romantic notion of walking to bed under the stars. These points gave Matt some distinct guidelines and an understanding of his parent-clients' expectations; but they also gave him a great deal of freedom in conceiving the fundamental form and lines of the structure. 'I wanted it to be an extraordinary place for them to retire to,' he says.

What Gil and Hilary wanted was a piece of architecture that was totally sympathetic with, and integrated into, the particular place in which it would be sited, as well as meeting certain needs, such as having shaded outdoor areas. Being on a hillside suggested shapes in sympathy with the natural contours that Matt, in his initial drawings, tried to follow. This meant that rather

The master bedroom on the ground floor has steps right outside that descend into the depths of the swimming pool.

The detailing of the ventilation shaft is reminiscent of Moorish decoration.

collection of rooms rather than the more complex distribution of rooms around a central staircase that is found in a typical British house. However, rather than expressing this linearity entirely internally, the design uses a combination of interior and exterior space to achieve a similar result in a modernist style. Matt also decided to construct the design in materials that would typically be used by Spanish builders – mainly concrete and metal. This meant that the building could be effectively realized by local workers. The result is a brilliant modernist take on a Spanish vernacular form.

Having come up with his conceptual drawing, Matt then handed it over to his father, who was going to act as the project architect for the build. Both he and Hilary loved the ideas that Matt had come up with. But it was also at this point that the cost-concerned client part of Gil started to make some changes to the initial design. 'So stingy old Dad comes in and says, "I can't afford it",' he laughs. '"I can't afford the cost of building so many separate dwellings. I've got to make it more rational and I can't afford two roofs!"' So on this basis he started working on more and more refined plans, rationalizing Matt's initial idea in terms of cost and making some other minor changes, while firmly maintaining the philosophy and most of the form of the original concept. He also concentrated on essential details, such as whether they had enough space to fit certain furniture in certain rooms, an exercise that revealed that some of the rooms needed to be increased in size.

But, of course, they still did not have planning permission for the plot. However, Hilary and Gil had started to take steps in order to get that permission. With the help of Paco, they had begun the process of getting their land classified as wet rather than dry, a local practice that

than a simple rectilinear form, the building follows the lateral curve of the slope. It is also on a terrace set into the hillside in seamless continuity with the other terraces below it. But the initial conception, one hinted at in the brief, was not one building at all but a series of three structures held together by one fluid, sweeping wall. These structures have intermediate spaces that are outdoor areas, sympathetic to the concept of al fresco life, and taking full advantage of the spectacular views. As well as attempting to integrate the building with the natural environment, Matt wanted to try to create a sense of continuity with the built environment – the architectural context of Spanish buildings. He says that this continuity comes from the way in which the organization of rooms in the traditional Spanish *finca* has inspired his design. This organization is based on a simple, linear makes it much easier to develop on. They had also had a meeting, organized by Paco, with a local planning officer at the town hall. He turned out to be a man with connections who was always helpful and seemed increasingly useful. Despite not speaking great Spanish, Gil was used to talking to people in planning departments and had a well-tested approach. 'Like all planning officers,' he says, 'there is a big bold front. You let him make a few contributions, you pick up the contributions that are positive, you drop the ones that are negative and suddenly it becomes half his idea and by that time you are on the road to him saying possibly yes.'

In order to get a definite yes, though, they had to submit plans in a formal application. This was not something that Gil could do himself as he is not a registered architect in Spain. Fortunately, they soon found a suitably registered Colombian architect who was willing to take on the design, and only five weeks after approaching him, permission for building the house on the upper level of the plot came through. 'And then we had Paco jumping up and down saying "When can I start?",' says Hilary.

The answer was 'fairly soon'. They negotiated a price of €284,000 (approximately £200,000) for the build with Paco, based on information provided by their Colombian architect, and he started almost straight away. By May 2003, he was project managing and constructing the build with a team of local workers. Hilary and Gil stayed in England at first and flew over to check on the progress of the build about every six weeks; later they visited as regularly as every fortnight. The whole thing, they say, has gone extremely smoothly – 'He's done a very good job', says Gil of Paco's work. That is not to say that costs have stayed true to the initial estimate, though. In part this is because they upgraded the specification of the swimming pool, adding a

further €30,000 (£20,000), and in part because of mistakes that were made by their architect in initially working out some of the costs. For instance, he had failed to take into consideration the cost of a waterproof roof – an omission that proved quite costly and which was not the only one. Hilary estimates that they are approximately 20 per cent over budget in all and that the total spend will be €370,000 (£244,000). But they do feel that the money is worth it; that it is a good investment. 'Our philosophy is that it is better in there than in the bank – or in a pension fund, for instance,' says Gil.

Looking at the finished product, it is hard to disagree about the sagacity of this investment.

It is a brilliantly conceived and elegantly executed building which has a sensitive engagement with both its natural environment and the built landscape in which it is situated.

This is evidently a complex relationship, though: it is a modernist piece of concrete and glass surrounded by terracotta tile-roofed *fincas*; a series of geometric shapes and lines placed among the smooth contours of a quiet rural valley. Yet the starkly linear shapes are entirely in keeping with a longstanding Spanish tradition and the three main 'blocks' (guest rooms, main living area, master bedroom and adjoining rooms) of the structure at the top of the hill echo the little hilltop hamlets of buildings that dot the landscape of Spain. The house is also far better thought-out in this regard than almost all modern developments in Spain, which in the main follow one archetypal design of the 'square villa' plonked indiscriminately on the countryside, regardless of the surroundings.

'I think we have deferred to custom far more than the modern developments do,' agrees Gil.

Sitting on a terraced hillside, the house manages to form a remarkable terrace in its own right: the downhill-facing side of the structure is an open veranda expressive of the space in front of it; the uphill-facing side a long, fluid line of wall expressive of the hill that continues to rise upwards. This long wall, which has been rendered perfectly, also has a wonderful curve that mimics the curve of the hillside itself and which, on the downhill side of the building, opens up an even greater panorama.

As you walk in through the front door – an imposing wooden entranceway with a Moorish feel to it – that immense vista is theatrically exposed by a wall placed directly in front of the entrance, though not quite enough to close off the view entirely. It gives you an enticing, sneak preview of the main feature. Walking around the

wall, the view opens up dramatically and continues to do so as you progress to the front of the tiled veranda, where the spectacle is revealed through 270 degrees across the hills and down to the sea. It is just one of many fantastic flourishes, details and surprises that this building has to offer. Some others include the oblique references to North African buildings: the square detailing at one end of the front wall and the ventilation stacks on the flat, tiled roof; the sensuous curve of the swimming pool, which is not treated as an isolated feature but a fully integrated part of the living space; and the great attention that has been paid to cooling in a building with so much glass and outdoor space.

It really is a fantasy building. Some of the fantasies that it embodies almost seem like clichés – for example, being able to wake up in the morning, walk two paces out of your bedroom and swim in a pool that has huge and fantastic views – but the way these fantasies have been realized are not clichéd at all.

There is a real freshness to the house; a zestful originality that combines modernism with a respect for vernacular architecture and specific location. In essence, it is a great piece of contextual building which has adapted to the tremendous possibilities of outdoor life offered by Spain's climate. That this end-product has been achieved is not just testament to the design, project management and construction skills of the various players in this project, but also to the organization and knowledge that Gil and Hilary have demonstrated about the whole process.

This has made it far easier to achieve their dreams and has made Gil a happy architect *and* a happy client.

OPPOSITE
The long, fluid sweep of the front wall facade is interrupted only by the single front door and square detailing at the near end.

BELOW
Square detailing on the front wall feels like a further nod to North African design, but also borrows from the design vocabulary of the Mexican architect Luís Barragan.

LEFT

Cool, modern and minimal. The unfussy approach to the interior of the main living space is a deliberate device to lead the eye outdoors.

PREVIOUS

The master bedroom has glass doors that look out to the pool, and windows behind the bed that light the room in the morning. Privacy is created by the half-mile or so to the next house.

ABOVE

The infinity pool was always intended to be an integral part of the design experience of this place.

Stairway to heaven:
Gil, Hilary and Kevin
stand on the spiral
staircase in the
corner of the main
courtyard. The design
was resolved by Gil in
consultation with the
Spanish builder, Paco.

The complex profiles
of this building – all
the angles, curves
and bits that stick
out of it – elegantly
illustrate the
intention of the
original design to
look less like a house
and more like a
small village.

The Japanese fashion designer Issey Miyake said in 1992 that 'design is not for philosophy – it's for life.' It's an epigram that should be etched on the brains of all designers, including – and perhaps especially – architects. Theory certainly has its place but the truth is that houses have to be lived in by people, and design is failing if it isn't helping them to improve their lives.

This is certainly the view taken by Jen and Derek Ray, a South African couple in their late thirties who say that 'lifestyle dictated the design of the house' that they've built in a ruggedly beautiful spot between Alicante and Murcia in southern Spain. Their attitude is that good design is something that enables them to live the life they want to with ease and comfort – hardly a controversial concept. And being able to build their own house has given them the opportunity to do this – to make a bespoke building that takes their idiosyncratic requirements into consideration. It is surely a better solution than the prevalent mass-produced housing – in Spain as much as the UK – that so often fails to provide good ergonomic solutions for most people, let alone more specific individual needs and desires. And the main motivation for the Rays was the desire for a home that gave them space and easy access to an outdoor lifestyle: a design that meant bringing the outside inside.

Being originally from South Africa, Jen and Derek were used to wide open spaces and large homes with swimming pools and tennis courts, so common among the white population. But,

PREVIOUS PAGES
Jen and Derek's house faces west into the setting sun – overlooking an enormous reservoir and with mountains in the distance.

after losing everything in that country, they have spent the last ten years of their lives in London, a notoriously cramped city. Indeed, the writer Paul Theroux said that 'the man who tires of London is tired of looking for a parking space.' Jen and Derek, along with their three daughters, were fed up with the close confines that they had to live in, as well as some of the other stresses and strains that London life has to offer. The land that they found to build their house on in Spain, though, has a horizon far enough in front of it to accommodate at least a couple of Londons. And in terms of parking, they've probably got enough room to squeeze in a fleet of number 38 buses! But they thought that they'd leave the buses in London, and park a house there instead.

The 8-acre plot has a small hill on its eastern side, with a road winding around it connecting the plot to the main road. Approaching on this small road reveals a dramatic view as you round the hill. To the west the land gently slopes down to a large reservoir about 400 metres away, which in the main has the appearance of a natural lake. On most days during the spring and summer the powerful sun shines pacifically off the water until it subsides and sinks below the distant hills, creating alluring reflections of amber, red, purple and pink on the surface of the reservoir. This large expanse of water has the effect of increasing the amount of light and emphasizing the impression of space, which feels vast. The fairly arid, scrubby terrain around the reservoir does not look too dissimilar to the South African bush, but it is also full of the Mediterranean aromas of wild thyme and rosemary.

However, it was the fantastic panorama that Jen found so enchanting and, in particular, the way that it is revealed as you approach the house. 'Suddenly that view hits you and you had no idea that it was there,' she enthuses. 'It's

amazing: all the expanse of water. With just one look around, we said "That's it".' The decision to buy was immediate; the estate agent even contacted the seller in Sweden by mobile phone while they were still on the site. Jen admits that she and Derek are very spontaneous people. But although a spirit of adventure is necessary in building your own house, an element of caution is also advisable. The one thing that the Rays failed to do before they bought their land was to check exactly what they would be able to do with it. If they had, they might have had some clue as to the planning nightmare that lay ahead of them.

The culmination of that nightmare – which lasted for three years – is described by Derek: 'I went to the town hall and sat on the floor in the corner of the chief architect's office with my head in my hands. I said, "I cannot believe that you can do this to me after three years."'

Things had obviously got pretty bad. Derek felt that he and his Spanish architect had been working for three years towards securing planning permission for the house, having discussions with the local council and making compromises with the design, only to be told at the end of it that certain things were not acceptable and that the council would be rejecting the proposal. Jen says that 'they seemed to change the goalposts all the time. One minute they were saying, "How many trees are you going to plant? Where's the gate going to be?" Then at the last minute, when they seemed about to give us permission, they turned round and said, "The building is too high".'

One of the main difficulties was that the couple were building in a conservation area – a place of outstanding natural beauty. But the few houses that can be seen from the site hardly seem to conform to design that is sympathetic

to the landscape. Those houses are also surrounded by ugly metal fencing that jars horribly with the surrounding countryside. So what was the problem with Jen and Derek's house?

Part of the problem was the fact that it was such an unusual design. And, to a large extent, that was because the design came from such an implausible-sounding idea, which Derek first had when he and Jen got married 17 years ago. It was an idea for their dream home. 'We actually had

plans for a house that we were going to build and it was a bit like Mickey Mouse's face,' says Derek, 'a giant circle with two little circles on top – double-storeyed with parapets – and a swimming pool that came from inside the house and flowed outside with little walkovers and views 30 miles either way.'

Perhaps the reference to Mickey Mouse is appropriate in that there is something rather fantastically Disney-sounding about this idea. But it is surely a design idea that is based on something that took inspiration from other buildings? According to Jen, the concept came from only one place: 'Derek's imagination,' she says. 'I didn't have any input on the whole thing; he just came to me with his idea.'

When they found the site, they realized that this was the opportunity to erect this dream home that they had thought about so many years before. But as soon as they began to look into it, they realized that the circular building was not a realistic option for a number of different reasons – in particular the difficulty of constructing circular walls, the problem of glazing in a circular house, and the challenge of installing furniture in such an unusual space. So Jen's idea was to facet the walls and create a polygon rather than a circle.

They got some help from a British architect who they had worked with before. The ultimate design consisted of a concrete-based structure comprising four interconnecting hexagonal blocks that, overall, form an approximately octagonal outline. The four hexagons also create a central space: a natural atrium which connects the different 'pods' together. However, the front (east-facing) and back (west-facing) of the building will also be clearly delineated with porticos.

On the ground floor both front and back open out on to patio spaces and, at the rear, there is a two-level swimming pool terraced into the natural slope. On the first floor there are balconies either side – for sunrise and sunset. But the desire to let the outside in has also been achieved by this multi-faceted building having views in every direction, particularly on the first floor where a large amount of glass lets light flood in and enables the Rays to enjoy the vast panorama. Being an active family, they also wanted a tennis court and extensive landscaping of the gardens that would include plantings of the locally abundant and prolific citrus trees.

Poised for the outdoor life... The large swimming pool begins to take shape. During the intense heat of the Spanish summer, plenty of the Rays' time is going to be spent here.

But the real *pièce de la résistance* of the building itself is the roof, a dynamic layer of concrete which contorts and cavorts above the structure below, held up by numerous columns of concrete that rise from the foundations.

OPPOSITE TOP
Rocking and rolling: this roof has a life of its own. Balconies at the front and back of the house, below the 'dormer' segments of the roof, provide great access to the spectacular views.

It is an unconventional roof for an unconventional building – relatively low at the front and rear edges, but with peaks over the balconies that look like dormer sections on a conventionally pitched roof. But the roof reaches its enormous apex in the middle of the building, with a cupola in the dead centre, above the atrium. It was the height of the roof in particular that seemed to be a problem for the planning people at the town hall, but Derek saw it as an integral part of the design that could not be changed or compromised.

'The design and structure of this house relies on the roof being that height,' he argues. There seemed to be no room for agreement. But at this point, with Derek sticking to his guns, the authorities relented, something that Jen puts down to his sheer and utter persistence.

'Derek's tenacity was incredible,' she says. 'I would have given up a long time ago. I think they actually gave us the planning permission because they were tired of us phoning. He would call and call and call. You could even hear them on the other end saying in Spanish, "Oh no, it's that Englishman again!" But Derek's enormous enthusiasm and energy, which are very infectious, must also have been factors.

It had taken three years to get the permission, during which time they were still living in London. Derek feels that if they had been in Spain they would have gone mad because of

the delay, but because they were going about their daily lives it didn't affect them as much as it could have done. In fact, he says, 'In many ways it was good; we saved like hell, we worked like hell, we put our business into a condition where it was saleable. The property values in the UK had escalated so we got even more money. It couldn't have worked out much better.'

In some ways Derek is being a little disingenuous here, as there was evidently a huge amount of stress involved. But surely the build itself would not be so difficult. In fact, Jen and Derek were extremely lucky in this respect. When they had bought the land they got a quote of about €385,000 (approximately £260,000) for constructing the house from a builder called Angel, who had been recommended to them by a friend. He was all ready to start and was simply waiting for the planning permission. But then, when it did not come through, Angel quite understandably became frustrated.

Because Derek trusted Angel and felt that he had given him a good quote, he wanted to stick with him. So, as a show of faith, he handed over €10,000 (£7,000). 'I said, "I am taking you at your word",' recalls Derek, '"If you walk away, I've lost 10k." And he honoured it.'

Angel has not only been the builder for the construction, but the project manager and, as the owner of a building supplies wholesale company, the main supplier as well. Once permission had been given in July 2003, work began on site in September, as soon as Angel and his men had finished the job they had been working on. And the build has proceeded with military precision due mainly to the exact co-ordination in supply of materials at the correct time in the build. Derek says that most days, after work has ended, a delivery of materials arrives and is unloaded for the next day's work, ensuring that construction starts first thing the

LEFT

The 'cupola' skylight will be glazed and inserted into the central section of the roof to provide light to the atrium below.

ABOVE

Putting the plexi-glass into the 'cupola' section prior to placing it into the roof.

TOP
Jen and Derek hope that the planting of citrus trees and landscaping around the house will help it blend more into the landscape.

ABOVE
Mixing cement in this heat is sweltering work: and there has been plenty of it to mix! This is a concrete-heavy house.

RIGHT
The perimeter walls were built from stone that has been reclaimed from the site.

following morning. It's a far cry from the negative image that Spanish builders in general seem to have in Britain and is proof, if proof were needed, that Spain has good and bad builders, just as surely as Britain does.

Although Angel has taken care of the project management, and done an extremely good job, Derek himself has been on site most days keeping an eye on the construction, making small changes where he felt they were needed, and doing some labouring himself. 'I took down poles and helped move things,' says Derek. 'I don't mind a bit of work. It was nice because you got to know the guys and you get a bit of input.' But this input, according to Derek, is merely minor tinkering and the client's prerogative. He is in no doubt that professional work is best left in professional hands; in fact, he sees that philosophy as an essential part of any type of project.

'Let the guys do what they do', says Derek. 'Let the builder do the building. Let the architect do his thing.'

And it seems that such an approach has worked. Derek and Jen certainly don't seem to have been at all stressed by their experience of building the house. And this seems mainly to be a result of the extremely stressful lifestyle that they left behind in London, where they worked like demons. But although they were financially successful, they felt they had sacrificed their family life to some extent in the process – something they are looking forward to curing in their new life in Spain. 'We wanted proper family life,' says Jen. 'And it's not too late for us.'

Once the construction had finished, Jen was determined to take control of the interior of the house, which she wanted to keep simple and practical, but also to include some exotic touches that combined old Moorish Spain and Moroccan influences. For example, a showpiece light fitting

The unusual contour of the concrete roof is seen clearly in this interior shot that overlooks the stairwell.

(a custom-made, North African style lantern) would take pride of place in the central atrium. She also used raw stone recovered from their land to clad internal walls and create a feeling of rusticity in keeping with the isolated position. This also gives a more natural feel to a building that is predominantly constructed in modern, highly processed materials. Somewhat paradoxically, though, the principal theme of the inside is the outside, which invites itself in through the large and numerous windows that wrap around the polygon structure. But these large windows also create the potential problem of huge passive solar gain, a problem increased by the fact that the house is in a completely exposed position with no shade except in the very early morning.

The glass itself is uv shielded and the roof provides shade by overhanging the windows. Nonetheless, this building is going to bake in the middle of the summer. Jen and Derek have countered this with an expensive, high-energy device: state of the art air-conditioning – really the only way to keep a building like this cool in the searing heat of Spain. But it is unfortunate that more thought wasn't given to how this building could ventilate and cool itself without the need for high-energy air-conditioning.

It could also be argued that a better design would have given more thought to how the building fits into the landscape that surrounds it. During the course of construction it was compared to many things: a squat origami toad about to jump into its pond – the reservoir – below, a stealth bomber ready to take off, and the inevitable alien-spacecraft-has-landed, are three examples. And the comparisons that the building invites are a clear indicator that it does not obviously relate to its environment. But at this point the place still looks like a building site and, over time, perhaps this building will become

more amenable to its surroundings, especially after the landscaping and plantings that Jen is intending: 'Although it looks like a big structure now, we're going to make it blend in much more'.

And, to be fair, this is all rather critical in the context of many of the other houses that litter the landscape in this part of Spain. Next to these, Derek and Jen's house has the distinction of being an incredible and outrageous prototype as opposed to an ugly and entirely mediocre example of mass-produced housing. And anyway, all of this is certainly not relevant to the Ray family who have built a home that is the successful culmination of a long-standing dream. It's also in a beautiful location that gives them acres of space and more breathtaking and sublime sunsets than most of us will probably see in a lifetime. And it is a family home that contains the amenities and provides the lifestyle that they could only fantasize about in London. In this sense, it is design that has succeeded.

But the building does have wonderful things going on inside it as well. The polygon shape means that there is an entire kaleidoscope of aspects that one can see from this house, bringing the vast and magnificent terrain into the rooms. The interior is spacious and varies in mood from the grand atrium with its high and spectacular cupola above, to the quirky little corners that are all around. It is a truly fascinating and unique place. Perhaps the most uplifting thing about the house, though, is the fact that you just know that the Rays are going to have a great time here, something that with their cheerful and exuberant attitude to life shouldn't be too hard. 'Enjoy for what you have now,' says Jen, 'because every day that has gone is history and you're not going to get that back. You've got to live in the now; there is no point in looking back into the past. We're living our dreams – what could be better than that?'

'Living the dream'...
The vast and
uninterrupted view
looking west from the
house opens up the
sky. That sense of
space makes it feel
a considerably long
way from London.

France

France contains most things that most people could ever want. Admittedly, that sounds like a pretty sweeping statement – and it is!

But think about it. It's the home of luxuries, including great wines, such as champagne and burgundy, exquisite gastronomy and sophisticated Parisian fashion. But it also contains some of the most devastatingly beautiful landscapes in Europe, including the mountains of the Alps and the Pyrenees, stunning rivers, such as the Ardeche and the Dordogne, and great seascapes – Brittany, for example. The opportunities for outdoor pastimes are huge, and France is one of the best countries in the world for skiing, cycling, climbing, walking and swimming. If you prefer a more relaxed lifestyle then the long lunches and vast array of fantastic beaches that France has to offer may be more appealing. And if you're a lover of architecture, the country has the most enthralling variety of vernacular styles, as well as some fine examples of church and secular buildings in modes ranging from Gothic to purist modernism. It's also a country with an intriguing and turbulent history, a nation of great literature and philosophy, art and culture. It would, of course, be difficult to list something for everyone, but the sheer variety of what is on offer in France is quite simply astounding.

The three builds that we're looking at in France feature three sets of people with very different agendas who've all found a place to build their dreams. One is in the Alps, one practically in the dead centre of France in Limousin, and the other in the south-west near the Dordogne river in the Lot *département*.

Limousin (La Creuse Build)

The quiet woods, rolling hills and pastures of Limousin offer a bucolic retreat largely free of many of the trappings of tourism and modern industry. This region, in the main part, offers a fantastic vision of rural France - quiet, sparsely populated and wonderfully unspoilt.

There is also easy access to the region via the airport of Limoges, which, at present, operates cheap direct flights to and from the UK.

The Lot (Martel Build)

The Lot *département* contains two major rivers - the Lot and the Dordogne. The Dordogne is infamous as the most Anglicized part of France outside Provence, and features some of France's most picturesque towns, including La Roque-Gageac, Sarlat-la-Caneda and Domme. One of the major attractions of these towns and those in the Lot *département*, such as Rocamadour, are their fantastic limestone buildings, many of which date from the thirteenth and fourteenth centuries. But the natural landscape of the area also has a gentle and alluring beauty. However, its great appeal also means that it is exceptionally busy in the high season, with lots of passing traffic - a possible downside for those seeking total peace and tranquillity.

It's also slightly awkward to get to by air because the main airports of Toulouse and Limoges are both at least a two-hour drive away.

The Alps (Les Gets Build)

The scenery of the French Alps is sublime, not only in the depths of winter when the snow conspires to highlight the grand majesty of the hills, but throughout the year. In the late spring and summer, the lush green pastures are exposed and the mountainsides lose a little of their austerity, replacing it with the dazzling brilliance of alpine flowers.

The Alps are obviously a fantastic base for skiing in the winter and for a whole variety of other outdoor pursuits during the rest of the year, but, unsurprisingly, it does get extremely cold. However, there are many resorts from which to choose a base, as well as some towns of outstanding beauty, such as Annecy. And what's more, access from airports is relatively easy: you can fly either to Geneva or Grenoble direct from the UK, leaving only short distances to drive into the mountains.

The medieval town of Martel is one of many richly historic towns near the Lot and Dordogne rivers.

France: Practicalities

France's immense size and diversity of physical landscape and climate offers enormous opportunities to explore all types of living. But it also offers a real challenge – is there one place in particular where you would like to live and that you think satisfies all your criteria?

It is easy to fall in love with a romantic vision that perhaps a holiday has offered, but if you are thinking about a permanent move, it's necessary to do an enormous amount of research. There are instances of people buying on impulse, successfully renovating properties and leading happy lives with relatively few problems. But you stand a far better chance of succeeding if you find out about where you are thinking of living in some detail before you move there, research the purchasing procedure, employ legal help and ensure that planning permission will be granted for the work that you are intending before you buy.

As with many European countries, the town halls (*mairies*) of France have far more power than in the UK. This makes a trip to the local authority (*commune*) an essential first step in any potential property acquisition, with a view to renovation or new build, as that is where the merits of your planning application will be decided. However, it's also true that this visit should help to ease your transition into local life: it's merely part of the etiquette when you move somewhere in France.

The purchase process

Selecting the property and researching it

Buying property in France is a popular pursuit of the British, and our love of renovating rickety old barns and farmhouses invariably arouses incredulity among the locals. Certain areas in France are notoriously popular – the Dordogne and Provence, for example. What this popularity means is that there is a wide range of sources for finding property. English broadsheet property sections often contain advertisements for French property, and there are numerous magazines about France that are good places to look. These include *French Property News*, *France Magazine* and *Living in France*, though there are also a number of others.

Similarly, there are numerous websites advertising French property, which are easily found via an internet search engine. However, if you have a specific brief that you want your land or property to fulfil, it is best to go through an estate agent (*agent immobilier*). This is particularly the case if you are looking in a very specific area. Estate agents in France are professional people who should be qualified, licensed and have indemnity insurance. They should also be able to provide a financial guarantee for at least €75,000 – about £50,000. Without such a guarantee they are not able to handle money, and any deposit should be paid to the notary or lawyer involved in the transaction. You can tell whether an agent offers this guarantee by checking that he has a bank acting as a guarantor – this information should be shown on his letterhead. He may also be a member of a professional body, such as the *Fédération Nationale de l'Immobilier* (FNAIM) or the *Syndicat National des Professionnels Immobiliers*. However, the ultimate benchmark of an estate agent's status is the *carte professionnelle* – every estate agent practising in his own right should hold this card and anyone who does not should be working for someone who does hold one.

There are numerous foreign agents working in France, many of them English-speaking. This in itself may be a benefit if you do not speak the language, though it is highly recommended that you do learn to speak French – there really is no substitute if you are going to go through the rigours of building in the country. But the fact that an agent is British may not bring any additional benefits and you should check his or her credentials with the same level of scrutiny as you would a French agent. Similarly, the agent should also be registered and either hold the *carte professionnelle* (which is very rare) or work with someone who does.

There is no fixed agency commission, but agents should list their fees, which normally range from 5 to 10 per cent, depending on the price of the property (the higher the price of the property, the lower the fee). The fee will normally be paid for by the vendor rather than the purchaser, and this figure is generally included in the quoted price for the property, listed as *commission comprise* or C/C. If commission is not included, the figure will be quoted as *net vendeur*. It makes sense to try to work with C/C prices as it makes matters a lot simpler.

However, agents are not the only property sellers in the French market. The notary (*notaire*), who is the person responsible for the legal conveyance of property, is also often responsible for selling it and is appointed by the vendor. You can also appoint your own notary to work on your behalf in checking the contract. Prices quoted by notaries for handling conveyancing are high – between 7 and 10 per cent of the purchase price, depending on the price of the property. This includes land tax, regional tax, plus VAT at 19.6 per cent.

You will find that there is a lot of scope for negotiation with property prices and it often pays not to accept the asking price but to put in a lower offer. If you have looked at a few properties and have taken note of the respective merits and downsides of each, this will make negotiation a lot easier, though if the original price seemed fairly realistic, you should not expect to get any more than 10 per cent discounted from it.

Because you will be buying the property as seen, without a surveyor's report, you ought to make some checks to ensure that everything is kosher before putting any money down. Even if you are taking on a ruin or simply buying land, you still need to check the land registry plan (*plan cadastral*) for the boundaries of the property and ensure that planning permission is likely to be given for the type of work that you are intending. On your side, you will want to get an idea of how much a renovation project of that building is going to cost before you invest any money in it and whether or not services are going to be easy to connect. It's at this point that you might want to get a local architect involved and get quotes from builders before you sign the preliminary contract. This, though, constitutes the absolute minimum that you should do. It would also be extremely prudent to check the local 'zone plan' (*le plan d'occupation des sols*) to check what zone your building is in, and the *certificat d'urbanisme*, which will show if there are any plans to build houses or roads nearby. Additional checks might include those for asbestos and lead within the building itself.

USEFUL INTERNET SITES
www.vefuk.com
www.frenchpropertysales.co.uk
www.1st-for-french-property.co.uk
www.propertyfinderfrance.net
www.frenchestateagents.com

Negotiations and contract

To ensure that you are protected at this stage, you could insert a conditional clause (*clause suspensive*) in the preliminary contract to the effect that purchase is dependent upon the granting of permission for the works that you intend to carry out. (Although it is legally shaky, you may wish instead to rely on an informal undertaking from the *mairie* that planning permission is likely to be given for what you intend to do.) You will need legal help in order to necessitate steps such as these and, although the conveyance of the property and the drawing up of contracts will be handled by a legal professional in the form of the notary, it is wise to employ your own lawyer who is proficient in French property law and who speaks a language in which you're fluent. French lawyers are called *avocats*. It's a good idea to compare quotations and, if possible, get a recommendation from a neutral party.

Assuming that all checks have been satisfactory, the notary will draw up a preliminary contract (*contrat de vente*), which is likely to be in one of two forms – either a *compromis de vente* or a *promesse de vente*. The former of these is the most binding of contracts, ensuring a commitment from both sides and stating property details, purchase price, completion date (usually two months after signing), conditional clauses and the status of the deposit in the event of default. But there is now a seven-day retracting clause in effect, during which time either party can pull out for any reason. The latter, much less common, form of contract is a commitment from the vendor agreeing to sell the property at a certain price for a period normally of three months, dependent on certain conditions specified by the buyer being met. However, it allows the purchaser to withdraw during that time if those conditions (such as planning permission being granted, for example) have not been met. This arrangement, though, normally means that in the event of default on the part of the buyer, it would also mean losing the deposit.

The deposit, which is paid upon the signing of the preliminary contract, is normally 10 per cent of the total price, paid either by transfer or banker's draft. It is essential that you understand at this stage what will happen to your deposit should you or the vendor default on completion. If you are in any doubt, do not sign the preliminary contract until your lawyer has clarified this.

After you have signed the preliminary contract, the notary will also have to take personal details from you in order to satisfy the complex machinations of French inheritance law. You should take legal advice at this stage as to whose name you should register the deed of the house under as it may have significant consequences later, particularly in terms of tax.

Post-completion formalities

Provided that any clauses you placed in the preliminary contract have been satisfied, you will be ready to complete within the timeframe specified in the preliminary contract (normally a maximum of three months, though there may be a degree of flexibility). The signing of the final deed (*acte de vente*) takes place in the notary's office, though a draft should already have been given to you in order for you to obtain legal advice. Either party can arrange for power of attorney if they are unable to attend in person. All outstanding monies – the balance plus notary's fees minus the deposit and any mortagage – are due at completion.

The one remaining step in the process is to make sure that your ownership of the property is registered at the land registry (*cadastre*).

Starting your renovation

You will, I hope, already have made extensive enquiries as to whether permission will be granted on your site, or perhaps you already have it. For any building occupying more than 170 square metres, plans have to be drawn up by a professional architect (*architecte*), who has to be responsible for the submission of a planning application.

Even if you are building or renovating a structure of less than 170 square metres, it is advisable to use an architect, particularly if he is from the local area and used to working with the *mairie*, in order to obtain planning permission. However, an architect can also be extremely useful for the duration of the project in terms of drawing up specific details for builders and other artisans. He may also be able to get better prices on certain materials and have useful contacts within the building trade. Ideally, you should try to get a recommendation for an architect, but if this is not forthcoming, you could find one by consulting the architects' professional body called the *Conseil National de l'Ordre des Architectes*.

Planning permission

In line with the fact that local authorities (*communes*) in France have a great deal more power than in Britain, planning regulations vary enormously from area to area, and individual decisions are not always entirely predictable. Rather than a statute book of regulation, you might say that there is a planning culture in each *commune* that has certain tendencies. In general, though, there is a lot of sympathy for the restoration of derelict old buildings, but only as long as certain procedures are adhered to.

Before you even look extensively in a particular area, it is worth acquainting yourself with the planning culture in the locality. And, as mentioned earlier, when you are thinking of making a purchase it is essential to introduce yourself at the earliest opportunity to the key decision-makers in the local town hall, giving them an idea of what building work you are intending to carry out. It is also wise to use a French, preferably local, architect who is used to working with your *commune*.

There are actually two documents that you need to have in order to start work. These are planning permission (*certificat d'urbanisme*) and a building permit, known as a *permis de construire*. If straightforward, these will be granted within two to three months of application; if rejected, though, new plans will have to be submitted and the process begins again. In theory it's best not to start building until you have your permission. However, in practice, many people already have an informal undertaking from the local mayor or planning officer, enabling them to start building before the formal permission arrives.

New builds are fairly strictly regulated in certain areas, such as the Alps, where you have to own an extremely large area of land before you are allowed to build anything on it. However, other areas, such as parts of the Massif Central, are very amenable to new builds and will often do their best to accommodate your plans to their planning culture, as they welcome the investment in their community.

Subcontractors

It is imperative to get a recommendation from a reliable source, references and see previous work of any subcontractors that you are thinking of hiring. Get a quote first. France still has a building culture of specialization, which means it's likely that you'll end up hiring a whole gang of tradesmen – stonemasons, plumbers, electricians, plasterers, etc. – on an individual basis rather than a main contractor to do this for you. Whether you co-ordinate these sub-contractors yourself – which can be tricky if you're managing the build from this side of the Channel – or get your architect to do this for you, is entirely up to you. A further option, though, is to employ a *maître d'oeuvre* – a combination of master builder and project manager – who will be able to provide expert supervision on a daily basis.

French builders will, of course, take long lunch breaks – often more than two hours – but learning to deal with that is just part of fitting in with a new culture. And long lunch breaks should be no barrier to ensuring that you end up with a quality product. That is achieved by hiring the right people, employing effective project management and having a realistic schedule.

need to know

|| **Estate agents in France should hold a licence, indemnity insurance and, most importantly, a *carte professionnelle*. Notaries (*notaires*) also sell property.**

|| **The vendor pays the estate agent's or notary's fees. Your own notary's fees can be high (7–10 per cent of purchase price) so need to be factored into the budget.**

|| **Check the boundaries of the property by looking at the land registry plan (*plan cadastral*).**

|| **Check the *plan d'occupation des sols* to establish which zone your property is in, and the *certificat d'urbanisme* to see if house- or road-building is planned nearby.**

|| **A *clause suspensive* in the preliminary contract allows you to pull out if permission is not granted for the work you are planning.**

|| **The most common form of preliminary contract is a *contrat de vente*, a binding document that ensures commitment from both sides.**

|| **A deposit of 10 per cent is usually payable on signing of the preliminary contract.**

|| **The signing of the final deed – *acte de vente* – usually takes place up to three months later.**

|| **French inheritance law is complex, so you should take legal advice on the name to be used for registering the deed as the tax implications can be significant.**

France: context and inspiration

France has a remarkable architectural heritage, a heritage that not only extends back for hundreds of years, but one that also has a very strong sense of looking towards the future.

It boasts some of the finest Roman remains in Europe, including the outstanding Pont du Gard aqueduct near Nîmes and the amphitheatre of Arles. Yet it is also the birthplace of one of the most revolutionary figures in modern architecture – Le Corbusier – and many modern public buildings are commissioned from leading European architects, including, from Britain, Richard Rogers and Norman Foster.

France has a remarkable and eclectic selection of church architecture. Perhaps the most impressive examples of these are the vast Gothic cathedrals, of which two of the greatest can be found in Amiens and Reims. They are spellbinding creations that arch toward the heavens, with little apparent effort, but great elegance.

The Renaissance influence in France is perhaps best seen in one of its most famous buildings – the Louvre in Paris. Many architects contributed to its various phases of construction over an incredible three centuries, but its overall effect is of an austere and supremely secular classicism. This former royal palace offers a massive contrast to churches such as the mid-seventeenth-century Sorbonne in Paris, an early representative of the baroque movement, which snowballed into the grand and ornate decoration of rococo. Later, in the mid-nineteenth century, such striking and sumptuous neo-baroque buildings as Garnier's Opéra were heavily influenced by this church style.

Just as it was in the very vanguard of modern art at the turn of the century, so France was also at the forefront of new ideas in architecture. Both the Eiffel Tower, built in 1889, and the work of Auguste Perret pointed to a revolution in architectural

The Louvre

The swimming pool on the roof of Le Corbusier's *Unité d'Habitation* in Marseille.

materials – in metal and reinforced concrete respectively – that would ultimately sweep across the world. A country that had long produced architects of vision, such as Etienne Boullée, France also had a visionary of the modern age – Le Corbusier – who was not only a brilliant architect but a strident propagandist. His modernist structures, hewn from a combination of concrete and revolutionary zeal, were to change the face of Western architecture irreversibly. And, although his visions of urban tower-block living may in large part have been discredited in the wake of high-rise failures in the UK, Le Corbusier is still regularly rated as the most revered architect of all time by polls of British architects.

In addition to these major architectural trends, though, there has existed a whole range of vernacular styles in different regions of France as a result of particular climatic and environmental conditions, local materials and historical circumstances. We'll have a look at some of those styles in the areas in which the builds we are featuring have been taking place.

The country house

The 'country house' is obviously a highly generic category that may include anything from a grand *chateau* to a lowly farmhouse. France is still a predominantly rural country, and there are thousands upon thousands of countryside buildings, which vary enormously from region to region.

In the Limousin, there is a strong historical tradition of building in the local granite. It is a tradition that cultivated an outstanding set of artisans called the *maçons de la Creuse*. They were stonemasons adept at working with the local stone, many of whom were employed by Baron Georges Haussmann in his rebuilding of Paris in the mid-nineteenth century. And Haussmann's impressive façades and imposing edifices can also be seen in some of the larger stone houses –

maisons bourgeoises – built in the Limousin region and which have similarly grand, though austere, designs. These nineteenth-century examples are built from large blocks of granite and are usually adorned with wrought iron.

In the Lot, by contrast, older buildings have an altogether softer appearance due to the fact that they were constructed in the pale local limestone. Many of these buildings date back hundreds of years, with towns such as Martel excellent examples of medieval architecture. Despite the stone having wonderful warmth, though, many rural buildings were built with defence from attack as an overwhelming priority. This is an area that was at the heart of the Hundred Years War: fortified hilltop towns, castles and houses with towers, set up on hills, provide testament to the turbulent past history of the region.

However, the majority of farmhouses in the Lot are built in local stone with red clay-tiled roofs, which, in common with much of southern France, are an almost uniform feature.

Warm coloured limestone is the main building material used in these rural farmhouses.

Ecological housing

The house built by Mark and Debbie Sampson as a grand design in the Lot was not built in limestone but in straw and wood. They were both very interested in designs not from the local area but, in the main, from the USA – straw-bale houses from Arizona and 'earthships' from Taos County, New Mexico, both of which have a distinct ecological component to them.

The earthship is a pioneering design, initiated by American architect Mike Reynolds, which attempts to function as an entirely self-sufficient structure and is made almost entirely from recycled materials. The main material used is old car tyres, which are rammed with earth and used as walls. The structure is dug into a south-

facing hillside, the tyres providing insulation, and a glazed wooden frame allowing passive solar gain. There are several innovative approaches to water collection and waste-water recycling, and electricity is provided by solar panels. Overall the earthship constitutes a radical solution to man's spiralling energy usage and its consequent effect on the environment.

The chalet

Apart from ski-resort apartment blocks, which are now generally discouraged by planning departments, there is really only one building style in the French Alps – the chalet. Emblematic of the area in which they are situated, chalets are built exclusively – historically at least – from the local materials of wood and stone. Normally consisting of two floors, the lower floor provides a stone support for the wooden frame above it. This in turn supports the enormous pitched roof, which protects the inhabitants from the large snowfalls in the area and enables melting snow to run off easily. Idiosyncratic chimney stacks with tops on prevent the snow from cascading down the chimney and on to the fire below.

The interiors illustrate a continuation of the marked simplicity shown on the exterior, with wood the dominant material throughout, in the walls, ceilings and floors, though these may also be stone.

A traditional old farming chalet in fresh snow, high up in the French Alps.

La Creuse, Limousin

There is an immense quiet here, 500 metres above sea level in what is almost the dead centre of France. Small, bright green fields adorned with the orange-brown Limousin cows are surrounded by thick, impenetrable forest. The only sounds are of gurgling streams and birdsong, with the occasional bark of a farm dog – it is a scene of pastoral seclusion. It is hard to imagine, then, that this area, only 60 years ago, was caught up in conflict and that a local manor house in a small hamlet was burnt down by retreating occupying forces. But that is precisely what happened to the house that Denise Daniel and Doug Ibbs bought in 2003; in fact, not much else had happened to it since.

The road on which the German soldiers made their barricade is shown in this site plan.

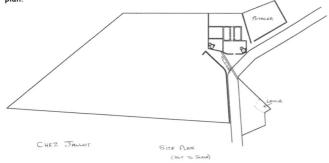

CHEZ JALLOT

SITE PLAN.
(NOT TO SCALE)

In 1944 German soldiers discovered that the house was being used by the *maquis* (French Resistance) as a regional headquarters. When troops came to investigate, Resistance lookouts gave the alarm and the house was evacuated before they arrived. An elderly man called Louis was a teenager when it happened, and he remembers the events well: he says that after the soldiers had burnt down the house, they searched the farmhouse where he lived, and still lives now, only 100 metres away. He and his family were hiding in the cellar. The soldiers found them but, having no evidence to link them to the *maquis*, they let them go. He says that a barricade erected by the Germans from casks of wine around the house cracked as a result of the intense heat of the fire. The gallons of red wine that flowed down the road towards his farmhouse must have looked like a river of blood.

Since then the area has changed relatively little, and the old house has stood as a derelict ruin for 60 years. That is, until Denise and Doug spotted it for sale on the internet and bought it almost immediately, despite the fact that they had not even been intending to buy property in France at the time.

'We were looking for a place in England,' Doug recalls. 'We'd just done up a house in Dorset and I was travelling an hour and a quarter plus to work, so the idea was to take on another project in the UK that was closer to work. But as we were perusing the internet we happened upon this place, almost on the same day that it was put on the web. We saw it on the Tuesday, phoned up and spoke to the agent and asked if we could come and see it. By Thursday we were on our way to France, on Friday or Saturday we saw it and by Sunday we had actually bought it.'

The couple met only six years ago at their local pub in Dorset. They are both 54 years old but seem to have the energy and sparkle of a pair

Chez Jallot: Denise and Doug's house, viewed across the flower-spotted pastures of the Limousin countryside.

of twenty-something newlyweds. This vigour and spontaneity is something that they showed in the dramatic purchase of the house, but it has also been an energy that they have needed to possess in abundance for what is really quite an enormous project.

The house is a nineteenth-century *manoir bourgeois* – a gentleman's country residence – that cost Denise and Doug £36,000. It is a huge and imposing building made up of large blocks of the local pale granite. It looms above the road in front of it, an implacable force three storeys high, brooding over all that stands before it. The impression of size is further emphasized by the fact that the ground floor is raised at the front to accommodate the slight slope that the house is built on, with double-sided steps reaching up to the huge front door. Below these steps there is the entrance to an enormous cellar, which occupies the entire footprint of the building. The main section of the house is divided into three – a hallway approximately 3 metres wide, containing the staircase, and two wings, each approximately 5 metres wide. There is a central granite balcony on the first floor at the front of the house with an original wrought-iron railing. The wrought iron is a motif that has been continued around the perimeter of the house, where huge, pyramid-topped pillars of granite are connected by spiked iron railings. The house is also situated in 1.6 hectares of land and has a barn adjoining it on one side; there is a large underground tunnel that runs below the road in front of them, and a giant loft space underneath the traditional sloping roof.

Neither Denise nor Doug had done a full renovation of a house before: they admit themselves that their previous project in Dorset was a makeover rather than a restoration. A challenge of this immensity, then, was quite a

Starting from the top. Stabilizing the structure began in the roof in order to pin the main walls together.

The crumbling surface of the stone was partly due to the intense heat of the fire in 1944.

place to cut their teeth. Doug remembers that 'it was pretty terrifying when we first came out here and saw it because the photographs don't do the place justice from the size point of view.'

But Denise recalls Doug saying that it was not too large. 'If it had been even bigger, it would have been a silly big project,' she says, 'but he looked at it and said that it was just about small enough to manage.' Considering the state that the place was in when they first saw it, that was a fairly optimistic conclusion. It had walls standing, but the beams within the building were mostly rotten, the roof had gone, it was structurally unsound and the entire site was overgrown.

The plan was not only to turn it into a home for themselves, but also to run a small *chambre d'hôte* (B & B), where guests can also have an evening meal with the 'hosts', with six rooms to rent. They were taking on the project management themselves and also hoping to do as much of the construction work as they could. It would have been easy to have looked at the enormous task that faced them and found it impossibly daunting, but they had the good sense to break it down and, as Denise says, 'When we took it on we said it's not one big job, it's lots of little jobs.'

Getting planning permission for the renovation was extremely straightforward. 'We went to the architect,' said Doug, 'he drew the plans. We ticked all the boxes. We submitted it. The builders started work and about three months later we got our planning permission. We were already well into the build by then. As long as the plans look alright and the boxes are ticked, then apparently there is no problem with you starting work.'

But their vision has not remained the same since the outset of the project, although more in terms of the interior of the house rather than any structural aspects. This is largely a result of spending lots of time in close proximity to the house. 'As you start to live with the house, you start to learn about the house,' says Doug. But they have also been influenced by speaking to neighbours who knew the house before the war and the family that had previously owned it. This knowledge of the building's history has given them an insight into the heritage of which they are now a part. That heritage, though, does not seem to be consistently remembered. 'When we talked to people they said, "Well, actually, it's really just a farmhouse", but local people, like Louis, said that the house was amazing: grand and lushly furnished.' This patchwork of memories has been fascinating for Denise and Doug. 'The basic vision was that this is a really

grand house, not quite Louis XIV, but it is going to be grand,' says Denise. But that grandeur had to be tempered to some extent by the demands of modern living, and there were also financial implications to consider.

When they decided to buy the house they worked out a detailed budget for the rebuild of £140,000. But that figure was based as much on what they could afford to spend as, up to a point, what they would ultimately achieve with the money. They began by clearing the site of the mass of vegetation that had grown over it. It was then necessary to stabilize the structure of the house. It had been built by one of the famous stonemasons of the area, a *maçon de la Creuse*, and in the main it had stayed remarkably stable. Some walls had come down, though, and on the tops of others stones were definitely loose and simply balancing on one another. Inside the house, structural damage caused by the intense heat of the fire needed repair. All this work required the expertise of a trained stonemason, so Denise and Doug recruited a local mason, Jean-Claude Ruchaud, to do the work. He began by putting up scaffolding on the sides of the house and then started to reinforce the structure and rebuild the walls. Once the top stones on the walls were in place, Ruchaud pinioned the two side walls together with a ring beam and concrete platform at the top of the building from where the roof could be constructed. He also sprayed the interior walls with concrete for further reinforcement, effectively creating a concrete skeleton for the entire building.

This was not something that Denise and Doug were entirely happy about – they did not want to use too many ecologically unsound materials in the build. 'But if you've got a structural problem in France the general solution is to throw concrete at it,' says Doug. However, they felt it was acceptable, not only because they

did not know of a viable alternative solution, but also because the outside of the building was keeping its granite walls, which were being repointed with lime mortar rather than sprayed with concrete. 'Also, we are recycling a whole house,' points out Denise, 'and that is surely environmentally friendly.'

Work could not start properly on the inside until the building had been waterproofed with some sort of roof. Their builder, Monsieur Grizon, went to work installing the wooden frame for the roof, which was going to hold dark grey slates that Denise and Doug had sourced from China. But at this stage there was a major delay: earthquakes and various other factors in China meant that their slates were late. Grizon and his men went to another job while waiting for the slates to arrive, but Denise and Doug climbed the

Without a staircase and floorboards, working on the second floor of a tall building was very precarious.

scaffold and worked themselves on repointing the stonework on the outside walls with lime mortar. However, this became impossible in the sub-zero conditions that they were encountering, so they decided to put up a temporary felt covering on the roof frame in order to concentrate on jobs that needed doing inside the house. The first of these jobs was removing remaining beams that were charred or rotting and replacing them with new ones, sourced in France, made from northern pine.

They were not experts in construction, but their attitude was to learn as they went along –

Some of the many cast-iron details that have survived years of neglect.

and have a laugh at the same time. And Doug says that, despite working extremely hard, it beats the hell out of what they were both doing before. 'We had both been doing fairly intensive jobs,' he says. 'I was driving 40,000 miles a year, and Denise was doing about the same. And just to get up in the morning, start work, have a cup of tea and chat is amazing.' But there were significant hardships and risks that they had to endure beyond the physical labour. Building sites can be extremely dangerous places, particularly when you are putting in beams where there are no floors and a daunting drop below. Doug had one fall and was fortunate to land safely. But it was a fright.

And all this time, with freezing weather in the winter, they were living in a small wooden cabin that they had erected on the plot. The cabin did not have a bath or shower and they even had to wash standing up. At Christmas they looked forward to going to a hotel so that they could have a bath.

They have found everyone friendly, despite, at first, having very little French between them. The fact that they have tried and make an obvious effort to speak as much French as they possibly can makes a big difference. Doug goes to a lesson once a week and has improved dramatically – during construction he was happy to give passers-by a guided tour around the site, heavily laced with numerous French technical terms that he has picked up.

They eventually gave up on the Chinese slates and managed to source others from the UK instead. Slowly but surely, the house began to take shape. This was especially noticeable when the windows were installed in March 2004, replacing the sheets of billowing blue plastic and delineating the form of the house with more clarity than had previously been seen. It began to look habitable – and it almost was.

They have had two very good contractors on site – the builder and stonemason – but were it not for Denise and Doug's determination and energy, this building would never have been built. Their indefatigable spirit and organization has ensured that things have happened in the right place and at the right time – a fine example of amateur project management. And they also seem to have massively enjoyed the experience. 'It is the most fun I've ever had,' says Denise. 'We laugh all the time. We love it.' And they also seem to love being with one another, essential if you are going to spend all day, every day on a building site together – which is what they have done.

The house is not finished but the building that they have now is a stunning transformation from the ivy-covered ruin that they purchased. They really have done a tremendous job, not least in the department of community relations, and their admirable research into the fascinating history of this building is a brilliant lesson in how to learn about the heritage of a place.

Once the windows were installed and the roof was up, the house really began to look the part. The substantial columns of granite supporting the railings at the front of the house are each one huge piece of stone.

Deni and Doug's taste
has come a long way
since they moved
here. The living room
is finished in 'French
Maiden Aunt's' style;
bourgeois, French and
very appropriate to
the house.

Floor by Deni,
staircase by Doug.
This is a house rebuilt
almost entirely by the
pair of them.

LEFT

**Rebuilding this house
in good faith has
meant using new
doors, fittings,
flooring and cornices
of the appropriate
design and size.
Furniture had to
be chosen with an
equally careful eye
for scale.**

ABOVE

**The large kitchen
is modern and
comfortably
furnished. The tiny
cornice bead seems
right for such a
modest room.**

LEFT
The main bathroom, plumbed by Doug and tiled by Deni.

Deni has decorated the bedroom with more French secondhand furniture. The result is charming.

RIGHT
Now it's finished, the house looks as though it may have been in constant occupation for centuries. The roof and lead gutters are restoration triumphs.

Bricks and mortar... steel and glass... raw lumps of stone – all building materials you might want to consider when constructing your dream home, depending on what type of structure you were after. But would you consider building with straw bales?

That's right – bound oblongs of dried, yellowish grass as bricks. 'Impossible!' you say. 'What about the fire risk? And surely straw does not have any strength or integrity as a building block? Remember the three little pigs?' Certainly in my dictionary, where the definition of straw is given as 'stalks of threshed grain, esp. of wheat, rye, oats or barley, used in plaiting hats, baskets, etc.,

or as fodder', no mention is made of straw being used as a building material: hats and baskets – yes; buildings – no.

But there are, in fact, many examples of straw buildings throughout the world – and it was a collection of such buildings that Mark Sampson and his wife Debbie, a couple in their forties, saw on holiday in Arizona, and which inspired them to build their house in the Lot in south-west France. After that first introduction to straw-bale houses, Mark was compelled to find out more about them, and was intrigued by what he discovered. 'The more I heard about them and read about them,' he says, 'the more I realized that they would make an ideal building material in some respects because of the insulation and that indefinable quality of well-being that they give. For instance, farmers have found that if they build their barns out of straw bales rather than concrete, their animals are far happier. It is also a waste product and it seems far better to make a house out of it than burn it.'

Indeed, one of the main reasons behind building with straw was the ecologically friendly and organic nature of the material. But it is misleading to say that the entire house is built from straw – in fact, the straw bales are fixed within a wooden frame that provides the main structural integrity for the house. Nonetheless, it is a radical design solution – particularly in an area of staunchly traditional buildings and a more modern heritage of relative conformity in house-building.

Mark and Debbie live with their daughter, Tilley, near the medieval village of Martel on the northern cusp of the Dordogne valley. The local pale limestone is the dominant building material here and there are many stone buildings in the area that have stood since the thirteenth and fourteenth centuries. However, Mark was determined that stone would not be his material

The simplicity of the design is clear from these drawings.

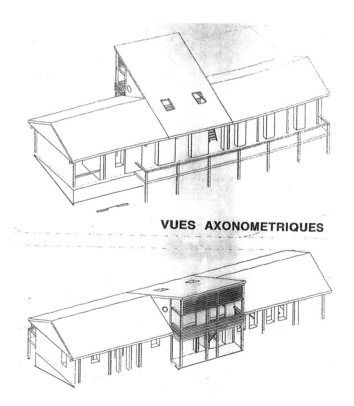

VUES AXONOMETRIQUES

The north-facing view from the house is vast and inspiring.

of choice. 'We didn't want to build in stone,' he says. 'Stone houses are nice; they're beautiful, but kind of cold. It is not a terribly welcoming substance, so I didn't want to do that at all, even though they look lovely. But I suppose by then we were also getting a bit blasé about the local medieval architecture.' He also saw the house as being a statement of individuality and wanted to avoid the modern French home prototype 'that are like little replicas' – in the same way that most modern housing in the UK is.

This is their second home in France. Mark and Debbie bought their first, on the edge of the Massif Central, after having been to France on holiday together only once. They had moved house from Brighton to Sheffield and, with the positive equity that they acquired from the move, decided to buy a holiday home. For a number of years it was precisely that, but ultimately their

search for a different lifestyle, a search for 'beauty and a better quality of life' led to a permanent move. Mark says that it was 'the tranquillity and the old-fashionedness' of rural France that appealed to them.

But they also felt that moving to France would be positive for Tilley, who had just been born – they wanted to bring her up in the countryside and thought that speaking two languages would prove a major advantage for her later in life.

However, they soon found out that, for them, the reality of living in France was quite different from going on holiday there – a salutary tale, perhaps, for anyone who is thinking of making the move abroad.

'Initially we went over for holidays,' says Mark, 'which gave us a false impression because everyone was very friendly and open and helpful

Mark hung tarpaulins around the outside of the structure to keep the straw dry as he put up the walls.

and it was a kind of adventure. But when we actually moved there we found that attitudes changed and that the original honeymoon was kind of over – it was more the reality of having to live there. Whether we were perceived as a kind of competition... I don't know. It was bizarre, but we found that people suddenly weren't prepared to help and offer advice.'

This led to them feeling isolated and upset that, despite their best efforts, they were unable to integrate properly with their local community. It was because of this feeling of isolation, perhaps, that they started forging links with other British people who lived a few miles from them in and around the Dordogne valley, links that ultimately enabled them to buy the plot of land on which they are building now.

And what a remarkable piece of land it is, due mainly to the fact that it has an absolutely stunning view. The panorama from the north-east-facing hillside has all the vast scope and romantic beauty of a Caspar David Friedrich painting, while displaying the full variety of landscapes that are so typical of this part of France: gently rolling agricultural land; tree-

shrouded, rounded hills; the deep and dramatic curve of the Dordogne valley. On the hillside opposite, a grand limestone chateau gives an indication as to some of the more spectacular local architecture. It is a sublime and beautiful place to build a house.

They found it through a British friend of theirs called Tim. He was driving past the site one day and noticed a 'For sale' sign, as well as the spectacular view. However, the entire site consisted of three lots and Tim wanted only one of them, but he also felt that he would like to know the people who were going to buy the other two. He therefore suggested to Mark and Debbie that they buy them and build their own house there. It was an idea that they had been thinking about for some time. They were particularly interested in ecological architecture and felt that building their own house would enable them to put some 'eco-friendly' ideas into practice. Not having any experience of design or construction, though, they needed to get some expert help. This took the form of a local architect called Gilles Faltrept, recommended to them by a French architectural advisory body because they felt he would be an appropriate person to work on such an 'alternative' project.

Debbie had already done some sketches of what she thought the end-product should look like. But they did not show these to Gilles at first. What they did give to him was a brief for what they wanted from the house. Mark describes this vision as being 'simple, elegant, with a lot of light and, of course, built with straw bales.' He adds that there were 'quite a few small factors, such as: somewhere to change our muddy boots near the front door, a balcony for the fantastic view and a mezzanine floor.' With what Mark calls 'remarkable serendipity' (or perhaps Debbie has missed her vocation!), the architect came up with a design that was incredibly close to Debbie's initial conception of the house – a design that they were both fairly happy with, if a little concerned that it could end up looking like a cricket pavilion!

Built with a sturdy wooden frame made from French Douglas fir, the structure is a fairly long rectangle, with a balcony running the length of the house on the north side and the magnificent view below. It is all on one level, with a tiled A-frame roof that is entirely conventional, apart from a mezzanine atrium that projects out of it halfway along its length on the uphill (south) side and which is pitched to coincide with the slope of the hill. This level also has a balcony that looks up into the trees at the top of the hill. The house has large windows – to maximize views on the north side – and passive solar heat gain on the south side. The front door is at one end of the oblong, with a wooden porch area in front of it – the place for all the muddy boots! So far it all sounds fairly conventional, until you realize that the walls are going to be made from straw bales.

When Mark and Debbie visited the houses in Arizona they felt a sense of well-being that they put down to being inside structures built from organic materials rather than concrete, metal

and fibreglass. But straw bales are also a practical building material in that they are lightweight, reasonably solid when packed firmly together, provide good insulation values and are able to be shaped into curves, niches and alcoves on the inside of the building. They are not left exposed but rendered over with lime or earth- based plaster.

Up to this point, Mark and Debbie's ecological credentials seem fairly sound. As well as using an environmentally friendly building material in the straw bales, they were also intending to use either a solar power or geothermic heat exchanger to provide their hot water, and tanks in the cellar that could be used for storing and recycling rainwater. Gilles had also designed in some element of passive solar heat gain with large south-facing windows, accompanied by good insulation to prevent heat loss. The one unfortunate thing about the position of the house is that the south-facing windows face uphill, and so get less light than they might otherwise do. Nonetheless, these self-sufficient mechanisms would decrease their reliance on utilities such as piped water and electricity – the aim of every environmentally friendly house builder.

But there is one problem with Mark and Debbie's eco-house – it is built on a huge slab of metal and concrete. This is the one thing that Mark seems to regret about the design of the house, but he sees it as a 'necessary evil'. 'I really wanted to do something with old tyres,' he says, 'but being totally impractical, I didn't think that I could offer us the kind of guidance that would create a solid base for the house.' Being on a hillside that slopes away fairly steeply does present a problem in terms of obtaining a good, solid foundation for a building. Mark ruled out the option of stilts because they wanted to have underfloor heating, for which they required a

The simple, rectilinear shape of the building can clearly be seen here.

'Sewing' the mesh. Twine is used to make the mesh cling tightly to the straw walls.

OPPOSITE
The use of wood and straw creates a tangible sense of well-being within the house.

slab. The other alternative, inspired by the 'earthships of New Mexico', was to build up recycled car tyres packed with earth. This solution would also have used some concrete, but not nearly as much as was ultimately poured into the foundations. It is, however, an extremely labour-intensive process, and there are also few examples of this kind of construction in Europe. Not having the right expertise was something that Mark was understandably concerned about, particularly in terms of conforming to building regulations.

'In an ideal world I would have spent longer looking around for people who shared the same vision, who could provide the necessary technical input that I lacked,' he says. But most of us to do not live in an ideal world, which means making compromises – Mark and Debbie have themselves and their daughter to house and have been living in a caravan throughout the summer of 2003 – one of the hottest on record – and a neighbour's gîte throughout the winter. Getting into their new house, making sure that it is safe and conforms with building regulations is their main priority; other than that, Mark says

that he can only do what he can 'and have certain abiding principles'.

And their compromise may yet be 'balanced out' to a certain extent – the other measures that they have installed into the design of the house mean that it should be more energy-efficient and self-sufficient than most homes. This consequently lessens the overall carbon-dioxide impact of the concrete production necessary for the foundations – or at least would do if France didn't already produce virtually all its electricity by nuclear power!

Mark confesses to being a born worrier and admits that it was not the best idea for him to appoint himself the project manager for the construction – 'I wouldn't recommend it to anyone of a delicate nature,' he says. 'I always hoped that someone else would take on the project management.' But, in the event, the task fell to him – the task of getting everyone and everything on to the site at the right time and at the right cost.

They bought the site for €25,000 and had a budget for the build that was the total price they had received for their last house – €146,000. Mark thinks that they will have gone over the budget, but not by a significant amount. The concrete base and wooden frame were the two things that cost the most amount of money – more than they had budgeted for. But the build has gone smoothly in most other respects. There was a delay first with the timber frame and then the delivery of roof tiles, which were very late indeed. This had the effect of pushing back the straw-bale walling, which could not go up until the house was watertight.

And the straw baling itself was not without problems. Mark had specified the type of bales he wanted to a local farmer: they had to be dry and as compact as possible in order to provide effective insulation and be easy to shape.

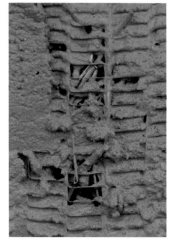

The continuity of a metal mesh – placed over the straw and timber frame alike – means that subsequent layers of plaster or render are consolidated and won't crack along the joint between bale and beam.

However, Mark was concerned that they were not compact enough. This meant that they were more difficult to shape, consequently placing more emphasis on good plastering to accentuate the forms of the niches and alcoves that he and Debbie had intended to incorporate into the building.

Overall, it has been a very stressful experience for Mark, but he also says that there have been 'moments of enjoyment and a sense of pride and satisfaction'. His advice for people who are thinking of embarking on a similar project is to 'think very, very carefully about it. Talk to a lot of people and have a very realistic picture of what is involved. In other words, don't go into it with rose-tinted glasses on.'

But he also thinks that it is desirable to try to integrate with the local community – something that not all Brits abroad are particularly good at. 'There is a whole breed of English expatriates who will buy their dream home and they'll make very little effort to actually learn the language,' says Mark. 'But I don't believe that this lets you truly appreciate the culture and the country, and to me there seems little point in doing it unless you're prepared to integrate to a certain extent, and that means that you have to achieve a

reasonable degree of fluency in the language and make an effort to adapt.' Although Mark believes that integration is desirable, he does not see his house as an expression of that integration but rather as a form of individualism. However, having originally been told at the Martel town hall that planning permission to build a 'wooden house' would not be granted, they submitted an application for the current design. Although the *permis de construire* took a little longer than usual, the application was passed without any problems.

And the project, with all its stress, has not stopped Mark from thinking about other building ideas for the future. Displeased to a certain extent by the compromises it has been necessary to make with this project, he would like to try a much purer experiment in ecological housing on the fairly large plot of land they now own.

'I would still contemplate doing it because we would have the security of the house that we were living in,' he says. 'I would want to do something even more environmentally friendly and much cheaper, as a kind of experiment. I want to see if you can really cut the budget to the bone and still do something that is environmentally sound and aesthetically pleasing using straw and wood and building on stilts, very simply, with a couple of big window openings.'

But the house that Mark and Debbie conceived and built on this spectacular bit of land is a wonderful family home. There is a special atmosphere of serenity and stillness inside the building due to the thick straw-bale walls that cut out low-frequency noise from outside. And the simple design expresses great strength through the fantastic Douglas fir frame, the main columns of which tower towards the ceiling. They give the place a feeling of solidity, and also reinforce the natural feel of the building.

It is also a practical building, designed to be lived in, with great outdoor balconies for the long, warm summers of south-west France. From the outside it fits well into the local built landscape, with its red-tiled roof in the traditional style, but it is also a manifestly different building from any of those that surround it. As an experiment in ecological housing, though, it deserves to be seen as a prototype rather than an unmitigated success. However, it does stand as a great example of building techniques that could be used in environmentally friendly houses, and design ideas that are working towards a self-sustaining dwelling – the holy grail of ecological architecture.

Mark, Tilley and Debbie are now able to spend large amounts of time on their balcony, enjoying the views and taking full advantage of the climate of south-west France.

The south-facing balcony on the mezzanine floor is faced entirely in softwood.

LEFT

The simplicity and purity of the end product are inspiring.

ABOVE

The main living area has turned out very spacious. Timber elements, like the staircase to the mezzanine, add a dynamic energy.

RIGHT
The thick walls and
niches are typical of
straw bale buildings
but the gently curving
profiles are also
suggestive of adobe
earth houses.

The guest room,
come Tilley's play
room; which, like
every room, opens
onto the vast balcony.

Mark's philosophy
was to build a
healthy house; free
of chemicals, full of
natural materials
and well-lit.

Debbie's study is the
ante-room to their
bedroom. Although
in, they still have to
unpack all their books
and belongings.

LEFT
The terracotta floor
conceals underfloor
heating – a relatively
high-tech solution in
a house that has
otherwise pursued
resolutely low-tech
methods.

Les Gets,
Haute-Savoie

Is there any better therapy than the mountains? Any greater antidote to the vicissitudes and shifting demands of the age in which we live than the beauty, majesty and immovable permanence of the hills?

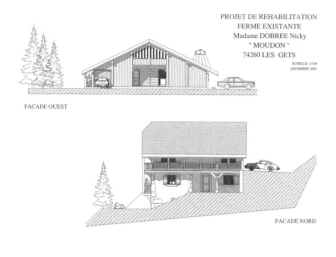

PROJET DE REHABILITATION
FERME EXISTANTE
Madame DOBREE Nicky
" MOUDON "
74260 LES GETS

ECHELLE: 1/100
DECEMBRE 2002

FACADE OUEST

FACADE NORD

PROJET DE REHABILITATION
FERME EXISTANTE
Madame DOBREE Nicky
" MOUDON "
74260 LES GETS

ECHELLE: 1/100
DECEMBRE 2002

FACADE SUD

FACADE EST

'The project of rehabilitating an existing farm'. Well, a fair bit more than that, really.

Alain de Botton wrote in *The Art of Travel* that 'what defies our will can provoke anger and resentment. It may also arouse awe and respect. It depends on whether the obstacle appears noble in its defiance or squalid and insolent.' Mountains almost always arouse the feeling of awe and respect that de Botton describes. Perhaps their manifest solidity places our own fears and insecurities in a humbling perspective: we're put in our place as mere specks in the vastness of time and the universe. And, in that sense, they allow us to think that our troubles are really rather petty, and human society, in general, undeniably ephemeral.

Whatever the philosophy behind it, the lure of the mountains was certainly irresistible for James and Nicky Dobree, a couple in their late thirties with two young children, who are renovating a traditional chalet in the French Alps. James was brought up in the mountains of Lebanon and learnt to ski when he was four years old – 'A lot of my early memories are of being in the mountains,' he says. Nicky's childhood was also rather unusual. She lived in many places across the world, including Vietnam, but mainly France, where she learnt to speak the language fluently. So, in retrospect, it seems almost inevitable that any mutual decision to branch out from their London home would have to satisfy two criteria: the mountains and France. And when you add a love of skiing to the equation, it could only really be the Alps.

But James and Nicky wanted their holiday house in the Alps to be a bit different from most others. 'I didn't want to have an ordinary chalet, like every other Savoyard chalet that you see,' says Nicky. 'The funny thing is that I've seen so many chalets and I haven't seen one – apart from in a magazine – that I want.' Haute-Savoie, where they have bought their property, does indeed have a relative conformity of building style. And recent planning culture has enforced that historical homogeneity to an even greater degree: modern houses have to resemble the traditional norm, even if the actual building techniques used do not correspond. So concrete structures are anachronistically clad in stone and wood and topped with the conventional pitched chalet roof that is so ubiquitous here.

There is more freedom with interiors, but these also follow some fairly strictly circumscribed variations on a theme. That central theme is wood – a material that is always in evidence here, not only in buildings and on the hillsides, but in the large troughs containing spring water that are made out of hollowed trunks, or the stacks of wood you see piled outside homes for putting on fires. One common interior style is that of cladding walls and ceilings with bright yellow new pine in what almost looks like a 'wipe-clean effect' – useful in a fondue food fight! As an overall finish, it's light, spacious and, in comparison to a lot of chalet interiors, modern in feel. But it also has a gaudy uniformity; the wood has no depth or discernible grain, and in many instances it might as well be plastic. The second common approach is that of the 'faux historical' interior in which new wood is made to look much older and darker through burning or staining, and the addition of traditional mountain motifs and objects – pine cones and pastoral flowers, for example – which are liberally sprinkled around the house as though to say 'this is a mountain chalet'. These elements combine to create a picture of the chocolate-box Alpine home, complete with distinctively carved wooden balcony balustrades; it's verisimilitude and, as such, treads a fine line between charm and unadulterated kitsch.

A house of two halves: the wooden upper storeys are supported by the stone base.

Traditional farming vernacular rules in Les Gets and most other areas of the Alps.

A quite different example of chalet interiors is the genuine, untouched article. There remain plenty of these in the hills, some dating back for centuries. Their wood shows all the genuine signs of age; it has been deeply coloured from years of exposure to smoke and heat and cold. The floors will often be stone – usually great uneven slabs – certainly in the kitchen and possibly in other rooms, or, alternatively, wide, ancient planks of pine. Interiors such as these give the feeling of being entirely surrounded by natural materials that have been hewn from the surrounding mountainside – which, of course, they have. In this sense it's a very beautiful and pure expression of man using the materials that surround him in a simple way to provide effective shelter and comfort in what can be a very hostile environment.

But James and Nicky wanted to do something very different from all three of these conceptions of the chalet: they wanted to build something chic, elegant and luxurious that combined Alpine materials with urban sophistication. That intention is perhaps what you might expect from a smart and cosmopolitan London couple, particularly as Nicky is an interior designer herself. But before they could start they had to find a place where they could apply this

Balustrades and log piles: common sights in chalet land.

vision. A new build, however, was out of the question because of the highly restrictive planning culture in the French Alps. 'There is a real restriction on the amount of space you can develop,' says James, 'so it's quite difficult and expensive to build from scratch. Essentially, you have to have an enormous piece of land that you can actually build on.' They were therefore looking for an old and fairly large building that they could strip the interior from and totally refit. Such buildings, though, are rather thin on the ground. James and Nicky had been looking for some time at the area around Les Gets, a resort about 50 minutes drive from Geneva airport. This proximity to an airport served by cheap flights from London was a major factor in their thinking – easy access is essential. And a house in Les Gets meant that, as Nicky says, 'You can do a day's skiing and be back at home for supper in London!'

However, access was not the only plus point they saw in Les Gets. It also has a massive skiing

The fine view from Ferme de Moudon looks out across the valley to the south.

area and an entire range of activities throughout the year that James and Nicky felt would satisfy the ever-increasing energy levels of their two young sons. 'The mountains are a great place to live all year round, not just a great place for skiing,' says James. In the summer, for example, the ski lifts in Les Gets are converted so that they can take bikes instead of skis to the tops of the hills. James and Nicky had also been to the resort enough times to realize that the place was beautiful throughout the year – not only in winter when the mountains are at their most majestic, but also through the other seasons.

So when an eighteenth-century farmhouse called Ferme de Moudon came on to the market, they went and viewed it with a local estate agent as soon as possible. And after viewing they decided to buy immediately, setting the process

in motion that same afternoon. It really was quite a find. It's a large, roughly square farmhouse building on a small road about a mile out of the centre of Les Gets, with magnificent views across the valley to the tree-clad hillside opposite. But higher up it is possible to see the vast bulk of mountains looming in the background, their peaks reaching toward the stratosphere.

As a consequence of being on a fairly steep slope, access into the house from the road is on the first floor – a floor built entirely of wood in a number of different forms, including an immense frame of great struts and beams for the pitched chalet roof, horizontal planks of cladding around the sides of the house and tall timbers like telegraph poles at the front and rear of the house. The ground floor, by contrast, is constructed from stone walls that have been

The chalet is situated on a small quiet road in a tiny hamlet. The *permis de construire* is pinned to the wall.

mortared together to provide a rudimentary foundation for the wooden structure that goes above it.

It's a very traditional piece of alpine vernacular architecture, unlike many of the buildings in the centre of Les Gets, which, as a resort town, has its fair share of kitsch follies, incongruities and theme-park Disneyfication. Despite the transitory and commercial appearance of the centre of Les Gets, though, it has a tight-knit community consisting of four main families who have lived in the town for hundreds of years. It is not a place that has sprung up as a result of tourism – it has merely prospered because of it. And the fact that, to James' and Nicky's knowledge at least, there was nowhere in Les Gets providing the 'top-end' chalet accommodation that they were proposing,

offered an additional incentive to the venture – making money. 'Having found the farmhouse, it was only over time that we thought, "Hang on a minute, we could do more than just own it",' says Nicky. So the idea of having the farm as a holiday home and also leasing it to the European jet-set was born.

'Sometimes these things fall out right, you know,' says James of the combination of reasons that led them to take on the project in the first place. 'It is definitely about having somewhere in the mountains. Then there is the French bit that is so important for Nicky, plus the design bit and the fact we both like to do entrepreneurial-type things: so the project satisfied lots of our different needs.'

But certainly one of the main interests in the venture for Nicky was the fact that she had the opportunity to be both client and designer in the re-imagining of a fascinating building. And, for her, 'There is nothing better than doing your own project.' She was particularly excited about the whole idea of people seeing a traditional-style chalet building from the outside, then being utterly surprised by the unconventional interior that lay within. 'You'll go inside and hopefully it will be the unexpected,' she says, 'because quite often these buildings are quite small and pokey inside, but we're trying to keep the whole flow of the space with materials such as glass, as well as wood and stone.'

The idea of contrast – in this first example between the outside and the inside – is one that Nicky wanted to sustain throughout the building by using a number of different devices. These devices included the juxtaposition of natural materials and their contrasting colours and textures – wood and stone, for instance. A further idea was to contrast light and dark shades, such as the dark timber cladding of the walls with lighter floors and furnishings. But Nicky also says that she wanted to work within the confines of the existing farmhouse – neither she nor James wanted to create a Manhattan penthouse in an Alpine setting, but a space where you still felt a definite sense of place. 'I aim to be as sympathetic as I possibly can to the building,' she says.

As well as showing an intention to preserve much of the existing basic structure ('Rest assured, anything old will still be there,' Nicky says), this statement would seem to indicate extensive usage of traditional materials – namely local timber and stone. But Nicky also wants to use much more modern materials, particularly metal and glass, as a further means of expressing contrast within the house. And the juxtaposition of these sharp, shiny surfaces with the natural solidity and chunkiness of great wooden beams,

for example, is a particularly effective and simple way of doing this. Techniques such as this also serve as a great statement of Nicky's underlying design philosophy. There is a purity and simplicity of approach mixed with a certain amount of epic monumentalism arising mainly from the whole theme of contrast. Not that Nicky would welcome such comments. 'It sounds a bit anal when you start trying to describe it too much,' she says!

Rather than trying too hard to describe many of her ideas, then, she carries a scrapbook with pictures of things that have inspired her in the formation of a design for the chalet. Chief among them is the work of a Norwegian architect called Henriette Salvesen, with whom Nicky has worked on the build. Coming from a country that combines a love of skiing with a fondness for timber architecture, it would seem obvious that a Norwegian architect might be able to contribute a different take on the interior of a French chalet. And, indeed, Salvesen brought with her an innovative angle of clean lines, contrasts and a

1990s sarking board but 1790s timber framing: Nicky had to deal with several earlier botched attempts at mixing the old and the new in this place.

This would be a view worth waking up to each morning.

sophisticated and luxurious living to a traditional chalet with a respect for the local materials, people and vernacular architecture. Preserving the basic structure, consisting of the stone and timbers of the original building, they have also imbued it with an elegant, modern feel using glass, metal and mod cons, which contrast with the evident authenticity of an old vernacular building. It has meant eschewing the rather dubious taste and design ethos of the tourist resort nearby, while being close enough to it to use its superb facilities. And perhaps the greatest facility that Les Gets offers is access to the mountains – the main reason for being here in the first place.

On certain winter days, particularly high up on the pistes above Les Gets, you can look down into the snowy valleys and at the immense escarpments all around, including Mont Blanc to the south, and the scene resembles a vast monochrome painting. The palette extends from the purest white of the snow through degrees of grey in the rocks and clouds to what appears to be the blackness of distant trees. The picture is one of contrasting tones, which combine to remarkable effect.

That symphony of tones, full of contrast and subtlety, is similar to the effect that Nicky has aimed for in the Ferme de Moudon. And just like the bright glare of the sun shining on snow, her interior should dazzle those who walk through the door into a chalet full of surprises.

Italy

Like France, Italy is always equated with a romantic and enviable lifestyle. When you think of Italy, you think of olives and wine, cypress trees and sunshine. Its smells are of basil and oregano; its sounds are the chiming of bells in grand cathedrals, the soaring arias of Verdi and Puccini, and its rapid and musical language. It's a country of stunning artworks, the great architecture of the Renaissance and the spectacular remnants of antiquity.

Another, racier, version might be the Italy of football, fast cars, modern interior design, fashion and sunglasses. Maybe trying to delve beyond these surface images and general perceptions is one of the motivations for people who choose to live in Italy rather than just visit it. But it's also true that people who do move abroad are often buying into a dream that is based, at least in part, on those images. After all, there is probably a great deal of truth in them.

And why not? A hilltop farmhouse in rural Tuscany, with views over a rolling landscape of sunflowers, vines and cypresses and within a short drive of the splendour of Florence or Siena, is many people's idea of the perfect home. Beyond the holiday-inspired fantasy, though, it's important to look at the practicalities of that place being your home all year round. Tuscany, for example, can have pretty harsh winters, while in the south the intense summer heat can be almost unbearable in July and August.

The region of Puglia is less well known to the British. In the south-east of Italy, in the 'heel of its boot', it has an entirely different feel from Tuscany in terms of climate, landscape and culture. Greece is only a short distance away by ferry, so the Hellenic influence is keenly felt, along with that of many other territories, including Spain, Turkey, North Africa and the Middle East. Whereas Tuscany seems to contain cultural reference points that have become central to western European history, Puglia feels as close as you can get in Italy to straddling the borders between Europe, Africa and the East.

There is great variety in Italy in terms of landscape, climate and culture. What is important, therefore, is to think specifically about the criteria that you're attaching to the location. Do you want mild winters or would you prefer to be close to the mountains in order to ski? Do you want to be able to get back to the UK quickly and cheaply by being near a budget airline destination? It's such questions, and many more like them, that you'll need to ask yourself in order to find the location that is right for you and your requirements.

Italy: Practicalities

As in much of mainland Europe, the town hall in Italy has a great deal of power – far more than in Britain. In practical terms this means that being on the right side of local people with clout is important, and over-reliance on the rational mechanisms of the law is a mistake.

It's vital that you have good relations within the community if you're intending any kind of major works that will need approval. The planning culture in particular is based upon this community-focused approach to politics. Efforts to reach out to neighbours and local people will invariably be enriching – not only in terms of your project – but on a personal level as well. It pays, in particular, to get in touch with the local mayor and the secretary of the local council: introduce yourself to them and discuss what you're thinking of doing. In rural communities especially they will be grateful that you're bringing an influx of capital to the area and providing jobs by recruiting local builders and other tradesmen, but the etiquette is very important and, if you get it right, greatly appreciated.

The purchase process

Selecting the property and researching it

As well as visiting at different times of the year, you can simply look in a magazine or on a website and decide on a whim that somewhere looks right – people do this all the time. There are now many magazines that specialize in homes abroad, such as *Italy*, *Homes Overseas*, *Homes Away from Home* and *International Homes*. You'll find advertisements for Italian property in all of them, though the majority tend to be for modern apartments and villas, which, if you're reading this, are presumably not what you're after! Looking in property and even travel supplements in British broadsheet newspapers, such as *Bricks and Mortar* in *The Times*, may yield some results as well. There are also increasing numbers of English-language websites

specializing in Italian property – though they understandably tend to concentrate on areas most well known to foreigners, such as Tuscany, Umbria and Rimini. The most obvious route to consider is to employ an estate agent (*mediatori* or *agenti immobiliari*) in the area in which you're looking. The benefits of having someone 'on the ground' are huge – it means that you can specify a brief for the type of property that you're looking for and be far more targeted in terms of locality.

Agents are either members of the Federazione Italiana *Mediatori Agenti d'Affari* or the *Federazione Italiana Agenti Immobiliari Professionali*. If they are not registered with either body (you can check this with the local chamber of commerce – *camera di commercio*), they will be liable to fines and will also not be entitled to commission (*provvigione*).

It's likely that you'll be asked to sign a standard contract with the estate agent before you look at any property. It's a good thing to do this at an early stage because haggling over terms once you have seen somewhere you really like is much more difficult. This contract is worth looking over carefully with a bilingual Italian lawyer (*avvocato*), though, as it will contain the terms of how much commission will be paid on the transaction and when this will be liable. If you have a contract with an *agenti*, only you will be liable for commission, whereas if you have a contract with a *mediatore*, both you and the vendor will be liable to pay commission. The amount is negotiable; however, the most that you would expect to pay as the buyer would be 5 per cent, while the norm is more like 3 per cent.

Once you have found a place that you're interested in buying, you may be asked to sign a document called a *prenotazione*, which is essentially a pre-contractual agreement to take the property off the market while you conduct the necessary checks and investigations. This will also require payment of a deposit – usually 5 per cent of the total asking price. This stage requires some care. It's essential that you make sure the *prenotazione* expressly states that the deposit is on account of the purchase price of the property in question, and that there are no restrictive clauses, such as no guarantee of commitment from the seller. Being asked to sign a document twice is a clear warning sign, as in Italy it's an indication of one-sided or unusual clauses being contained within an agreement. It would be prudent, once more, to ask your lawyer to check this document. You should also clarify with him as to whether he feels it's necessary for you to sign such an agreement, or whether it would be possible to move directly on to the next stage.

In Italy, both parties to a prospective transaction are required to act in good faith. So before any legally binding contract is accepted, the seller should pass over to the buyer a copy of all documentation that relates to the relevant property. He should also inform you of any material fact that may influence your decision to proceed with the purchase. You should, at the same time, make your own investigations about the property. This includes employing a surveyor (*geometra*) to undertake a survey – if applicable; do local land registry searches (to confirm the ownership of the building and whether the owner is legally entitled to sell it); and check with the local authorities (*comune*) as to what local planning and building regulations apply to the property. This last aspect is obviously of massive importance: planning laws are strict in Italy, but also very localized. You need to find out what the specific policy of the local *comune* is and have a reasonably clear idea about your intentions for the site. Planning permission is discussed in more detail overleaf; finding out at this stage what's likely to happen, though, is helpful before you make a definite commitment.

It's also strongly advised that you check on third-party rights. These are particularly applicable in agricultural areas, where farmers and other neighbours often have priority in the purchase of agricultural land offered for sale.

USEFUL INTERNET SITES

www.italy-real-estate.net
www.live-in-italy.com
www.umbriaimmobiliare.net
www.interitalia.biz
www.rural-retreats-italy.com

Negotiations and contract

When all searches have been satisfactorily completed, the terms of the contract (*compromesso*) will need to be agreed: in particular the price, amount of deposit and date of completion. Usually, a draft contract will be produced before the final contract is drawn up.

A notary (*notaio*), who is a government representative in property transactions, will draw up the contract. It is advisable that you do not use a notary recommended by either the seller or the estate agent: this is the buyer's prerogative. Using someone who is independent of the other parties involved will go some way towards ensuring his impartiality.

The contract should be submitted to your lawyer for close inspection before signature. However, you should make sure that it includes the following:

|| **A detailed definition of the property that you're buying, preferably with a scale plan attached.**
|| **The total price of the property and amount of deposit payable, with an attached receipt upon payment.**
|| **A statement of intent from the vendor agreeing to the legally binding nature of the sale of the property on or before the date of completion.**
|| **A resolution to any problems that were discovered in the searches conducted.**

Upon signing the contract, you'll also be liable for the deposit (*deposito* or *caparra*), which will be between 10 and 30 per cent of the total price of the property. The status of this deposit, such as what happens in the case of default in completing, should also be defined within the contract and is something that you should seek clarification on from your lawyer.

An additional charge is incurred through the notary, who will demand a fixed fee of 2.5 per cent of the official registered selling price of the property, payable upon completion.

If there is likely to be a substantial amount of time between exchange of contracts and completion, there is the option to safeguard your interests by registering the contract with the local registration tax office. This protects you from the possibility (and it has been known to happen) of the property being sold by an unscrupulous vendor to multiple purchasers. However, it does also mean that you may end up paying a higher rate of Italian registration tax (*imposta di registro*) upon completion.

After the exchange of contracts, some further steps are needed in order to complete the purchase. These will take place at the notary's office. The vendor will need to produce the title deeds and all relevant planning and building licences. If you're not going to attend the completion yourself, you need to organize power of attorney (*procura*) for your lawyer – or another party – to attend and sign in your place. You'll also need to obtain an Italian tax code number (*codice fiscale*), which you can do by visiting the local tax office in person with your passport.

Funds are normally delivered by banker's drafts (*assegni circolari*), which need to be organized in advance of completion and include relevant taxes and the notary's fee. Once payment has been made to the satisfaction of the notary, the title deed (*rogito*) should be handed over to you, identifying you as the owner of the property.

Post-completion formalities

After completion you should be able to collect a certified copy of the purchase deed, which should be available from the notary's office after a period of two to three months.

Formal notice of change of ownership should also be given to the local police authorities (*questura*), using a form supplied by the notary.

You'll then, finally, be in a position to think about building, or getting on with the renovation of the property that you now own.

Starting your renovation

In order to start your renovation or new build, it's likely that you'll be employing an architect to help you with the design, and it's essential that you do so for drawing up plans that must be submitted to the local *comune* for planning permission.

There are two distinct types of architect in Italy – an *architetto* and a *geometra*. An *architetto* is what British people would generally understand to be an architect – he will be someone who has been trained for five years at university level, and will have studied design and architectural history. The *geometra*, on the other hand, has been educated at somewhere akin to a technical college and is a mixture of a surveyor and an architect.

Under Italian law a *geometra* is qualified to design buildings up to a certain size. But if you have a clear understanding of what you want and simply require help in formalizing your ideas and having plans submitted for planning permission, then a *geometra* should certainly suffice. If you're renovating a listed building, you'll have to use both a *geometra* and an *architetto*.

Probably the two most important things are to have a personal recommendation from someone whom you trust and to have seen previous work by the person you're going to be employing – whether a *geometra* or an *architetto*. It would also obviously be preferable to employ someone who has demonstrable experience of working on a similar project to the one that you're undertaking, and it is essential to obtain references.

You should be able to obtain guidelines for the fees of both an *architetto* and a *geometra* – a complex table that will give the fee as a percentage, depending on what type of project yours is. This table should be made available to you at the planning office.

Planning permission

The one expectation that you should certainly have about gaining planning permission in Italy is that it's not going to be the same as planning permission in Britain. The complexity is largely due to the fact that local authorities have far more power than in Britain, meaning that a lot more decisions about planning are made locally. There is no uniform legislation that covers the whole of the country, but innumerable local policies guided by national legislation, which is, theoretically, fairly strict. It's entirely possible, as in the case of David and Leonie in Puglia, that you'll have to build 'illegally' and then apply retrospectively to the authorities for a *condono* – literally, a condoning of illegal building. This is a pretty scary prospect, but commonplace in many parts of Italy. However, it can also be expensive, with the *condono* being charged per square metre. The best advice is to check what the local policy is in advance and in as much detail as you can. It's also important to get an idea of what kind of costs you're likely to incur in this process and how these are going to impact on your budget. Each *comune* has a surveyor (*geometra*), who should be able to give you guidance on these issues. But 'policy' is not always what actually happens on the ground; this is often as much about fostering good relations with neighbours and the relevant people at the *comune*.

However, there are some national regulations and guidelines that you should also be aware of. If a house is located in the historic centre of a town or village, it will fall under the auspices of the Ministry of Cultural Patrimony (*Ministero per i Beni Culturali*). In this case, the property is declared to be part of the country's *vincolato* (register of listed buildings) and all plans must therefore be approved by the ministry.

The often strict planning laws now encountered in Italy are a reaction to the laissez-faire planning regime of the post-war years that saw a lot of non-contextual architecture springing up. Very commonly, you have to own a minimum amount of land before you're allowed to do any new building on it. So in many places the buyer of a ruin is allowed to build only on the exact 'footprint' of that structure. Usually a totally new build is not an option, and what you can construct is very strictly regulated. Policy varies in different parts of Italy. In the *comune* of Ostuni in Puglia, for example, the local *geometra* estimates that 40 per cent of new builds are in fact illegal, but end up being granted a *condono*: a far higher percentage than in somewhere like Tuscany.

need to know

|| The purchaser pays commission in Italy, between 3 and 5 per cent of the property or land price.

|| Once you have seen a property in which you are interested, you may be asked to sign a *prenotazione*, a pre-contractual agreement, to take it off the market. Discuss with your lawyer (*avvocato*) whether this is really necessary, depending on the circumstances.

|| Beware of being asked to sign a document twice. It may mean there are unusual or one-sided clauses in an agreement.

|| As well as the usual checks, make sure you also investigate third-party rights on the property, particularly in agricultural areas where neighbours often have priority in purchase.

|| Before any contract is drawn up, the seller should provide you with copies of all relevant documentation and also tell you any fact about the property that might influence your decision to buy.

|| The contract, *compromesso*, is drawn up by a *notaio*, a government representative in property. Try not to use a *notaio* recommended by either the vendor or estate agent. The contract should then be thoroughly checked by your lawyer.

|| A deposit of 10–30 per cent is payable on signature of the contract and the balance on completion, usually by a banker's draft.

|| The notary will also be paid a 2.5 per cent fixed fee on the purchase price, payable on completion.

|| Consider whether you should register the contract with the local registration tax office, a safeguard should your vendor turn out to have sold the property to more than one buyer. This could increase the amount of registration tax on the property.

Italy: context and inspiration

Italian architecture is immensely diverse and rich in history. Cities such as Venice, Rome and Florence contain some of the most visually stunning and enduring examples of Western architecture ever to have been built – buildings such as St Peter's in Rome, the Doge's Palace in Venice and Brunelleschi's celebrated Duomo of Santa Maria del Fiore in Florence.

Two thousand years ago Italy was at the heart of the Roman Empire, an empire that assimilated and proliferated a classical architecture from the Greeks, which has possibly had a more profound effect on architecture in the Western world than any other single influence. Italy was also the birthplace of the Renaissance, which forged new links with the country's ancient classicism and communicated its new, vibrant culture to much of the rest of the Western world through structures designed by Andrea Palladio, Donato Bramante, Jacopo Sansovino and others.

Italy was unified as a country as recently as 1876. Before that time it was composed of a number of different states with their own identities – identities that even today have not been entirely forgotten. Indeed, Italy remains fiercely regional in many respects, including its own local traditions, and this to some extent is reflected in a variety of regional vernacular styles that have evolved in response to local materials, climates and the many different peoples that have populated areas of Italy over the centuries.

The defensive requirements of any traditional Italian town or village meant that they were placed on hilltops within fortified walls.

Tuscany

During the fascist regime of the 1930s, Tuscan vernacular architecture was seen by many cultural commentators to embody the essential qualities of Italian design. For example, one critic writing in 1933 noted 'the admirable proportions and perfect geometry of these humble buildings, the virile and sweet harmony of the walls, and the effect of the precise dimensions with this exceptional native skill'. There is some justification for believing that Tuscany is central to the evolution of Italian culture in general – the modern Italian language evolved from a Tuscan dialect, for instance, and Tuscany was the wellspring of the Renaissance. And just as the classic countryside of Tuscany, with its rolling hills adorned with vines and cypress trees, seems the quintessential expression of Italian landscape, so the rural buildings dotted around on picturesque promontories appear the archetypes of Italian country architecture.

Tuscan farmhouses are normally simple structures composed of fairly uniform geometric shapes, with Roman-style clay tile roofs, and often containing a courtyard surrounded by arched windows and doorways. Stone and brick are regular building materials, usually left unrendered on the outside, while the traditional interiors of these buildings are generally near-identical, with cream or yellow lime-washed plaster walls, terracotta (or sometimes stone) floors and red clay-tiled ceilings with oak or chestnut beams. They possess charm and beauty, but many Tuscan farmhouses also reveal in their design a certain amount of fortification and safeguards against possible attack. This was a very real prospect for landowners over many centuries in Tuscany. Whereas the last time Britain was invaded was in the eleventh century, Italy and its historically constituent states have been overrun many, many times – and frequently by one another.

The promontories on which many of the farmhouses sit are usually man-made and produced with the specific intent of being able to see danger from a distance. Many buildings also have one or more towers for the same purpose – indeed, this is one of the most distinctive features of the Tuscan vernacular.

In the heartland of the Renaissance it's also common to find evidence of classical motifs being used even in buildings such as farmhouses. There are often loggias, arcades, cloisters and columns to be found in rural buildings, and even the occasional example of grand Palladian symmetry and proportion infusing the simpler rural vernacular. In this sense, Renaissance architecture is not only to be found in the great cities; its influence is keenly felt throughout Tuscany.

Fortified settlements are invariably high-density. Today, the architectural density of Italian communities seems charming and theatrical.

Puglia

In Puglia, two very characteristic types of building are *masserie* and *trulli*. *Masserie* are whitewashed cubic structures that, like a great deal of Pugliese architecture, look as if they could belong in North Africa, or even Greece, as much as in southern Italy. There is a strong sense of 'otherness' about these buildings; they do not fit with much of the rest of traditional Italian architecture, and vary from anything that you might see in Tuscany.

A heterogeneous form, they range from humble farmhouses to grand *palazzi masserie*, though they do share many generic characteristics. They are all constructed from the local calcareous tufa stone, and present tall and daunting façades, with few windows and flat roofs. Behind the façade there is usually a main building and a collection of living quarters and other outhouses within high perimeter walls that also contain a square central courtyard or cloister. The outside walls of the buildings are usually whitewashed, but the interior reveals raw stone and brick-vaulted ceilings. Carved stone finials, rather like minarets, are a common decorative motif on the corners of the flat roof, further emphasizing the link with North African and Arabian structures. This link is largely a result of the vast number of Mediterranean populations that have washed through Puglia over the centuries: in towns and villages in the region you can clearly see the influence of the Turkish, Greek, Spanish and Arabic invaders and colonizers of old. The fact that Puglia was often overrun by armies, bandits and pirates is a key feature in the design of the *masserie*. Within their walls agricultural workers were able to band together for protection.

Likened to inverted ice-cream cones or lids from Moroccan tagines, the quirky structures called *trulli*, scattered around the Puglia countryside, invite a whole array of strange comparisons. The most famous *trulli* site is in Alberobello, but they are also sprinkled liberally throughout much of the region. They are idiosyncratic, conical-roofed stone buildings that have stood in the area since the nineteenth century, though their origins are obscure. They are similar to buildings found near Aleppo in Turkey, a similarity that has led some people to believe that they were constructed in Puglia by an immigrant ethnic group. More widely believed, though, is that they were first conceived of by indigenous people accustomed to working with the tufa limestone that is so abundant in the region.

Trulli are fairly primitive structures built entirely of stone – even the conical roof does not have a wooden frame, but is built up of concentric rings of stones that get smaller and smaller as they rise up to the pointed top. Each row of stones rests on the one below, and it's the resulting inward and downward pressure alone that keeps the roof in place.

They are fascinating and alluring buildings; and there is something indefinably 'cute' about them – it's lovable architecture. They are also increasingly popular to buy, and most estate agents in *trulli* areas will have properties to show at any given time.

For lovers of quirky buildings, *trulli* might make a fascinating project.

Brancialino, Tuscany

You want to leave behind the daily grind: the stresses and strains of modern city life, of commuting, meetings and staring at a computer screen all day – you would like to live a more peaceful existence. Howard Smyth and Janne Hoff-Tilley faced just such a scenario. In 1999, both in their early fifties and living in London, they realized that they didn't want to do the hard-boiled city lifestyle for the 15 years or so that they had left before retirement. And it was Howard's lifelong ambition to restore an ancient building – but in Ireland rather than Italy.

PREVIOUS PAGE
King of the castle. Il Castello Brancialino (centre) stands proudly on a promontory, with exceptional views all around.

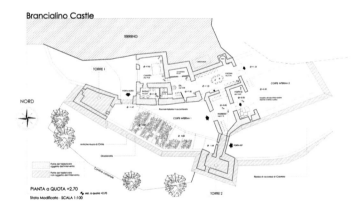

Brancialino Castle

The plans give some indication of the complex topology of the castle.

That dream came about because of a trip that he took when he was 18 years old – a trip that led him around Ireland, stopping at castles, monasteries and chapels along the way. But it was also not just a vague, intangible dream – Howard had identified a particular place that he wanted to purchase and restore all those years ago. 'I wanted to buy a tower house on the edge of Loch Corrib, about 15 miles north of Galway,' he says. 'And finally, come the moment when we wanted to stop working in London, I went in search of the owner.' The property was not for sale, though, and by the time Howard had found a ruin that was on the market, Janne had decided that the Irish climate was not the best in the world to retire to. 'It's much nicer in Italy,' she says, 'because the sun shines!'

Ireland was Howard's passion but, 'being a decent chap', as he says, he agreed to Janne's wish to investigate the possibilities of buying in Italy. They began by looking at a website he saw advertised in *The Sunday Times*, and the very first time the two of them logged on, they saw what was to become the focal point of their lives for the next four years – Il Castello Brancialino, an ancient castle that the website itself described as being 'not for the weak-kneed'! Not being particularly weak-kneed types, they were interested enough to go and see what it looked like. So only a couple of weeks after first seeing the castle, they were in Italy.

The castle is in Brancialino, a hamlet a few miles outside San Sepolcro, a fairly small town on the eastern edge of Tuscany, best known as the birthplace of Renaissance artist Piero della Francesca. Indeed, two of his most well-known paintings – *The Resurrection* and *Madonna della Misericordia* – still hang in the town's civic museum, and the old master's presence is felt everywhere within the town. The castle is situated in the hills above San Sepolcro, on top of

its own small promontory, high above a dammed section of the River Tiber. The view from the place is remarkable – with grand mountains towering up to the east, dense forests and open fields on hillsides to the south-east, the broad, glassy stretch of the Tiber to the south and rolling hills away to the south-west. It's a vista largely unencumbered by other buildings or, indeed, much other evidence of modern human life. It's unspoilt, wild and beautiful.

At that first viewing, though, the castle itself was romantic and beautiful only in the sense that it was a total ruin where dreams of splendour could quite happily grow – a fertile ground for impractical idealism as much as the weeds and ivy that thrived there. But Howard Smyth is not an idealistic dreamer; he is a practical man.

Before he embarked on this project Howard was a management consultant who rescued sinking companies. 'You can be a consultant to the company and offer them advice – which they'll probably ignore anyway,' he says of his methodology, 'or you can join the company as the managing director and change the business from within.' The second option was Howard's preferred way of getting things done, so it seemed inevitable that this hands-on approach would be carried on in the rebuilding of the castle, particularly when he had an immediate grasp of the possibilities inherent in the place. 'I could see the potential straight away,' Howard says, 'how you could design it; what one had to do.'

But he and Janne also felt that it was in a

The fortified walls of Il Castello Brancialino emerge from the trees. Six years ago they were densely covered in undergrowth.

It's impossible to exaggerate how much earth, debris and vegetation Howard had to remove. Even now, all the walls still need to be cleared of roots and repointed.

superb location, with a bar and restaurant within walking distance, a fairly sophisticated town – San Sepolcro – less than 6 miles away, a number of major Italian cities – Florence, Bologna and Perugia – within an hour's drive, and other places of interest – Assisi, Urbino and Arezzo – also close by.

And so it began. Howard and Janne realized that it would be a massive task to rebuild the pile of ancient stones that lay about the site back into the grand castle that the stones had once been part of, but they had no reason to believe that it would turn into the complex, messy, leviathan of a project that it eventually became.

To start with, it took a year before they were the owners of the site. Negotiations were difficult due to the fact that there was a sitting tenant, meaning that they had to deal with her as well as the owner of the property. Tenants in Italian law have far more rights than in Britain, and the financial consequences for Howard and Janne were significant – they paid £35,000 for the castle itself, but had to pay £70,000 to the sitting tenant in order to obtain outright ownership of the land. However, this period of time was also useful for them in order to form more detailed plans, check that permission would be granted for the work they were intending, and work out

their budget. They allocated a fairly large sum of money – £300,000 – to the building work, a sum that they had accumulated through the sale of their house and Janne's business in London.

The building was in its dilapidated state mainly because of an earthquake in 1930 that had caused devastation to many buildings in the area. It was also subsequently blown up in the Second World War by the German army. But, according to Howard, it was the earthquake that had done most of the damage. And during the course of the renovation project, it must have felt like the tremors from that seismic upheaval 70 years ago were reverberating through history to try to prevent the castle from ever being rebuilt.

The first *geometra* whom they employed to work on the project was sacked after a year because Howard and Janne said that he had not produced the necessary drawings or submitted anything to the local planning committee, as he agreed he would. So they replaced him with a new *geometra*. This time, however, something far worse happened, which led to the whole project being jeopardized. Unfortunately, Howard did not realize this for quite some time. Building work began on the site in September 2000, with Howard and his builder, Claudio, believing that the planning committee from the local *comune* had seen all the relevant plans and approved them. What happened in February 2001, then, was a massive shock. A delegation from the local council arrived on site and asked Howard to explain what was going on: they said that they had not authorized the work that was being carried out. Howard produced the permits that had been given to him by his *geometra*. It was at this point that the *comune* delegation told Howard that the permits had been forged and that permission had not been given for the work – it was illegal. 'It really got into a hell of a mess,' says Howard. There were

'forgeries, falsification of community papers... just about everything'. And as for the *geometra* himself – well, he landed in serious trouble. 'There are six criminal charges that he is going to have to face, and I think 23 professional misconduct charges,' says Howard.

As a shock, this was fairly high on the Richter scale. And the fact that illegal building work had taken place had serious consequences, even more so because of the fact that the castle is the equivalent of a grade I listed property in the UK – part of Italy's *vincolato*. This unhappy state of

affairs then led to censure from the Pieve Santo Stefano *comune* and the threat of an enormous fine – approximately £130,000 – almost half of Howard and Janne's entire budget for the project! Things really had gone very wrong. 'I felt like saying, "You can just have the whole lot back,"' says Janne.

Inevitably, if they were to do it all again, they would take more precautions to begin with. Howard's advice is pragmatic and eminently practical: 'Take out references on the particular people you are going to use and – if you do not

The window arches begin to take shape high up in the living room. The loggia will extend outwards towards the tower that rises four stories from the base of the castle.

speak fluent Italian and do not understand planning – find someone who can translate.'

But they decided to continue with the project and at this point the situation began slowly to improve. In the first instance, the local authorities recognized that the situation Howard and Janne found themselves in was not ultimately their fault. They also recognized the fact that they were injecting capital into the area and creating short-term jobs for builders working on the site. The sympathetic attitude displayed by the authorities led to the penalty eventually being reduced to £3,000 – the absolute minimum the *comune* could fine them – and the understanding that most of the building work already done would be allowed to remain. They

also pushed to get the planning through committee stages in order that work could restart on the site as soon as possible.

However, 'as soon as possible' was not very quickly at all – in fact, the due processes that had to be carried out before work could continue would eventually take almost two years – two years of a dream lying in tatters on a rubble-strewn hillside. But Howard was determined to carry on doing something. So he moved himself into the one (barely) habitable part of the building and lived there on his own for a year, spending the time moving the great stones that littered the site. Through the winter it was freezing cold inside the castle. During the day he must have felt like Sisyphus who, in Greek myth,

The concrete floor and the new cement-built arch are concessions they had to make in conforming to earthquake regulations.

was punished in Hades by having to roll a heavy stone up a hill for all eternity – a futile and thankless task. But Howard says that if he ever felt in doubt about what he was doing, he would walk to the top of the promontory and look at the view: 'That is what it's all about.'

And really the energy and determination that Howard has demonstrated displays Promethean vigour rather than Sisyphean futility. After stealing fire from Olympus, Prometheus was chained to a rock, where an eagle savaged his liver until Hercules freed him. Now Howard may not have been having his liver eaten by a large bird of prey, but he was certainly extremely relieved when the builders were finally allowed to move back on to the site and thus improved his predicament no end.

The *comune* had granted approval in December 2003, when Howard had paid the £3,000 fine in full at the town hall in Pieve Santo Stefano. Building work then began in January 2004 when Claudio, who had been distraught over the effect that being involved in illegal building works might have on his reputation, returned under the guidance of a new architectural team – this time an *architetto* and a *geometra*.

The aim of the build was to achieve a sympathetic restoration in a traditional regional style. It meant first of all having to piece together what the castle would have looked like before it was destroyed, something that was achieved both by looking at the remaining wall lines, which had almost uniformly remained intact at the base, and researching into local archives for information about the property. It soon became clear that it would be difficult to rebuild the castle in a pure, original manner due to the fact that there was no truly original building and it had been added to over many centuries. The oldest standing section is estimated to be

eleventh century, but major portions were also added in the thirteenth and fourteenth centuries, while one part of the castle was built only about 1840. As a piece expressive of architectural purity, then, it would not hold together. The aim instead was to try to reinstate the building to its zenith state – the fullest extent of the castle before it had been destroyed in 1930.

It's a fairly complicated site topographically as well as historically. Approaching from the north side on the only road to the castle, you notice two main buildings on the promontory – an old church on the left and the castle to the right. From this angle, at least, the castle does not have quite the size and grandeur you might expect. However, the building derives much of its mass from the fact that it's built on a steep slope, and looking at it from the opposite direction – the south – its presence and sense of scale are substantial and imposing. The ramparts at the base of the castle have a great deal to do with this – their stony bulk rises to perhaps 7 metres in places. The impression of a fortified building is further emphasized by the two tall, vertiginous towers that are such an integral part of this building. All this, of course, is very exciting: it's a castle, a real castle!

LEFT
Special 'earthquake bricks' are designed to absorb vibration.

ABOVE
The roof design and materials conform to the local historical canon.

It's thought that there were once definitely three towers, and maybe even four, but permission for full restoration was sought (and given) for only two of them. The most striking of these is the south tower, four storeys tall, and connected to the rest of the building by a bridging section, which, on the first floor level, is a loggia that opens out on to the west side. This arm, which stretches out as though from the body of the main building, is connected back to what is the real centre point of the castle – the spectacular living room, which has windows all around and, in particular, two large arches that expose the grand vista, which takes in the River Tiber below. Light dramatically floods into this room, but further back in the building, especially on the ground floor set into the hillside, there is much less light. The interior is very dynamic in this respect: although the whole orientation of

the castle is towards the south, there is a wide variety of light conditions.

The interior is mainly decked out in traditional Tuscan style – large wooden beams on the roof (*trave*) are divided up with smaller beams (*traverti*) underneath a red-tiled ceiling. The floor, in the main, is laid with terracotta tiles, giving the whole place a wonderful, authentic Italian feel. This impression is enhanced by the motif of arches that begins in the lower main gateway near the base of the ramparts and extends to the ancient arched entrance in the wall between the main living area and the west tower, the windows of the ground-floor dining room and first-floor living room.

But the construction has been complicated by the fact that anti-earthquake measures have had to be employed to try to prevent a repeat of what happened in 1930. These included using a special kind of brick that soaks up vibration. On the exterior of the building these have been covered with stones, and on the inside they have been plastered over. But anti-earthquake precautions have also involved using a massive amount of concrete in the build – something that is not in keeping with the sympathetic nature of the restoration. It's the kind of thing that would make the woman from English Heritage poke herself in the eye. But for Howard and Janne there was no other option. Taking such precautionary measures is essential in earthquake zones – not only for the safety of the building and conformance to building regulations, but also to get compensation from the State in the case of an earthquake. If your building hasn't been built with the correct materials, you won't get a euro for any damage.

But all of this has not come cheap. Howard and Janne have not exceeded their original £300,000 building budget by much, but it's all the other things – renting an apartment while

OPPOSITE
The new and the old:
the wall containing
the arch is among
the oldest parts of
the historically
chequered castle
while the block
adjoining it was
only constructed in
the mid-fourteenth
century. Howard and
Janne have repaired
or replaced all the
stone windows in
the building.

the castle was being built and legal fees, for
example – that have meant this exercise has
become an extremely expensive one.

What they have ended up with
is something very special. Owning
a medieval castle in Tuscany
really is the stuff of fantasy.
Il Castello is a magnificent and
monumental building. But it has
a more subtle beauty in the way
that it's contoured to follow the
shape of the hill in a slight curve,
the wonderful arches, spectacular
loggia and the classical Tuscan
interior. All these things would be
wonderful anywhere; what makes

this building particularly amazing
is the incredible vistas that it
presides over. But having the
additional satisfaction
of sympathetically reviving an
ancient building that might
otherwise have been lost to
history must also be pleasing.

And then there is the triumph over terrible
adversity... well, yes, but was it really worth it?
Howard seems to think so. 'The end result is well
worth the wait, the effort and the heartache,' he
says. 'The cost... well, that's another thing that
we may never reconcile. But the principles of the
thing are absolutely right, and I think that we
have been totally correct to be patient.'

VIETATO
L' INGRESSO
AI NON ADDETTI
AI LAVORI

LEFT

The jutting posturing of this building is impossible to escape – its history is firmly rooted in conflict, its character unflinching in its strength.

ABOVE

Janne has no need to let down her hair! She and Howard are jointly looking forward to reaping the rewards of years of patience and hard labour.

Wherever possible,
Howard and Janne
have kept and
repaired existing
stonework such as
these time-worn
steps.

TOP RIGHT
The couple's
architect, Gino,
wanted to stain all
the woodwork but
Howard and Janne
were having none of
it. In the end, old
wood is left old and
new oak and chestnut
are put in as new.

RIGHT
The south tower
retains an
authentically
fortified appearance
with few windows.
The scaffolding
conceals the
connecting loggia
that runs between
the living room and
the tower.

OVERLEAF
The striking Tuscan
landscape, as seen
from the hills above
San Sepolcro.

Ostuni, Puglia

OPPOSITE
**The simple stone
sentry post at the
top of the cave has
similarities with
local *trulli*.**

storing and pressing olives. Around the buildings were three principal walled garden areas, and a perimeter wall encircling the majority of the farm. The plot is on a gentle slope that opens out into a dry stream-bed at the bottom.

The couple are financing the project with the sale of their Tuscan home and art school, which gave them a total budget of approximately £165,000. With the plot costing them £140,000 – more than they had initially intended – it meant that they had very little money (£25,000) left to convert the property into what they wanted it to be – both a home for themselves and an art school for visiting artists.

That vision involved creating enough accommodation to house guests, as well as bringing together the disparate elements of the plot in order to give the place an overall feeling of unity and harmony. In simple terms, they wanted to provide a working place for artists, somewhere that would both inspire them and enable them, in a practical sense, to run the school.

David was responsible for most of the design. He says that he wanted to try to blend the plot in with the natural architectural features of the

landscape – the prominent rocks and the huge, antediluvian olive trees that are hundreds of years old. Part of this process, he says, is making it seem as though 'the buildings are emerging from this great plateau of stone and looking organically part of the country'. This obviously meant using the local tufa limestone as the principal building material. The approach is reminiscent of the way that the old town of Ostuni itself looks, having the appearance of being contiguous with the natural landscape, rather than in violent contrast to it. This seamlessness is also apparent between the interior and exterior of buildings, in the way that raw stone is left exposed and plastered inside rather than rendered over.

'I wanted it to look as though it has always been here, and to do so within a local vernacular,' David adds, 'but there will also be some more contemporary structures, for example, sunshades on verandas that are modelled on the vaulted ceilings, reflecting the shapes and forms of the place.' The overall philosophy behind the design, then, has been organic, and sympathetic to the surrounding landscape, materials and architectural heritage – a personal Eden in a local vernacular.

The plot as they bought it, though, presented itself more as an archaeological curiosity than a building site and potential home, with the two houses in states of dereliction and almost all of the garden and perimeter walls crumbling, or in total ruin. In addition, the buildings had been rendered in ugly grey cement that seemed to have no place in David and Leonie's vision of natural rock organically emerging from the surrounding landscape.

But what an archaeological curiosity! The vast cave underneath the mill house contains flat beds that have been cut into the rock, probably for housing seasonal workers. Rising out of the

**The cave where the
olives were stored
and pressed has
been cleaned in
preparation for a
new role as studio
or gallery.**

The accommodation block makes extensive use of pitted, calcareous stone, similar to the bedrock, and softer tufa limestone in the arch detailing. Both give the building an almost archaeological character.

The covered portico at the front of the building provides shade to retreat into during the heat of the day.

Ireland

If Ireland, as one ex-prime minister of the country said, 'is where strange tales begin and happy endings are possible', you might think it sounds like the ideal place to contemplate building your own grand design.

And it seems apposite, in a great nation of storytellers, to be plotting your own adventure with a cast consisting of your wonderful family, a brilliant architect and builders from heaven. The ending is like some emerald green dream, heavily laced with lashings of black and white genius. Whether the yarn turns out happily, though, is only in part up to you; just as in the rest of life, building projects have a common knack of complicating the crystalline plot and sharply defined characters you started out with.

Not that there's anything in Ireland – except, perhaps, the weather – to stop your vision from becoming reality. It's a magical country with stunning mountains and coastal scenery, verdant rural tranquillity and the fascinating artefacts of a turbulent, if often troubled, history. It's also a history that has an intimate and complex relationship with Britain.

However, Ireland is not just the stuff of history lessons but a thriving, youthful society looking to the future and helped no end by its legendary 'Celtic Tiger' economy and a determination to be at the very heart of the decision-making process in Europe. That's despite the fact that it has one of the smaller populations in the EU and relatively few major urban centres outside Dublin. Indeed, Ireland's quiet, largely undeveloped countryside means that it's possible to escape with ease to peaceful and isolated locations. In addition, there are plenty of ruins – from churches to fortified tower houses – to take on, should you have the inclination.

It's also a great place to get to and from Britain, with budget airlines operating a number of routes, and fast, regular ferry services sailing from a few British ports, including Liverpool, Holyhead and Stranraer.

So perhaps it's time to contemplate that 'strange tale' then, if you haven't done so already. We're looking at the story of two people – Andrew and Jackie – who did just that and took on the renovation of a ruined nineteenth-century church on the beautiful west coast of Ireland.

Ireland: Practicalities

The Republic of Ireland has a couple of obvious practical advantages over the other countries featured in *Grand Designs Abroad* as a place to buy property or land and undertake a building project.

The first is that English is the primary language in Ireland (albeit unofficially), rendering the potential problem of getting lost in translation one only of possible cultural rather than linguistic difference. The second is that many procedures – such as the purchase process and obtaining planning permission – are similar to those in Britain and largely without the onerous bureaucracy found in some European countries. The main downside may also be recognizable – the weather. But this familiarity should not lure you into a false sense of security. Research and planning will be key to the success of your project in Ireland, the same as everywhere else.

First, you have to find where you want to build, and although the Irish landscape may not have quite the same diversity as some other countries, it still offers a great range of beauty, particularly in its coastal scenery. This varies from sheltered sandy coves to splendid, craggy peninsulas, islands and coastal mountains, while Dublin, on the east coast, is a dynamic and sophisticated major European capital. Different parts of Ireland offer different attractions, including the remote isolation of much of its countryside and the warm conviviality of many of its towns and villages.

The purchase process

Selecting the property and researching it

Just as Ireland's economy has experienced an economic boom in the last few years, so has its property market. It means that there are plenty of sources for finding property and land, but it also means that prices have been hugely inflated and bargains are few and far between. British broadsheet property supplements, such as *Bricks and Mortar* in *The Times*, may turn up some results, but Irish newspapers and magazines – the *Irish Independent* and *Irish Post*, for example – are also worth a try. A better solution, though, is to have a look on the Internet, where there are a number of websites containing Irish property and land for sale.

The other alternative is to use an estate agent. This gives you the option of specifying a particular brief for a particular area: highly recommended if you would ultimately like to get what you started off wanting. Estate agents are often rather confusingly called auctioneers in Ireland, despite the fact that auction only accounts for approximately 10 per cent of all property sales. But auction is a traditional form of transaction and all agents have to hold either an auctioneer's licence or house agent's licence, although these are no guarantee of the estate agent holding any form of relevant professional qualification.

Unless you specifically employ an estate agent to act on your behalf, all commission on a property will be paid by the vendor – sometimes called the lessor. If you do specifically employ an estate agent (which shouldn't really be necessary), you should ensure that the rate of commission is confirmed in writing before viewing any land or properties.

Just as in Britain, a solicitor is essential in property transaction whether you are buying at auction or by the most common method of private treaty. Finding a solicitor should be reasonably simple, but ideally you should try to get a recommendation from a trusted contact. If you're in any doubt, it might be a good idea to contact the Incorporated Law Society (www.lawsociety.ie). Your solicitor will be able to check the title of the property and whether any particular planning or zoning issues affect it. Just as in Britain, your solicitor is also essential in the conveyance of the property and will check the terms of contracts and handle their exchange in an almost identical way. Their costs are generally 1 per cent of the price of the property plus VAT (currently 20 per cent) and expenses.

Once you have found a property that seems suitable, you should commission your own survey (rather than one from a mortgage provider, for example) to make a detailed check of its condition. At this stage you might also want to bring in your architect – if you are using one – to make an evaluation of the property. In addition, it's recommended that you conduct enquiries with the local authority as to whether they think planning would be authorized for the type of work you're intending. This in large part depends upon the development plan for the local area – a public document well worth looking at with your solicitor before you commit to any sale.

USEFUL INTERNET SITES
www.myhome.ie
www.iavi.ie
www.keyproperties.ie
www.pbutler.ie
www.independent.ie
www.propertyfile.net

Negotiations and contract

In the most common form of property transaction – private treaty – property prices are generally given as negotiable figures, and you may be asked to provide written offers. As in Britain, it's probably unwise to make too low an offer, although with ruins in particular these are more likely to be accepted than with a 'normal' transaction for a second-hand property in what has been a very strong market. This in part is explained by the fact that people are far more inclined either to new-build themselves or buy modern property built in the last 25 years. Nonetheless, making a very low offer could freeze you out of the picture altogether.

If there are any provisions attached to the offer – that it's dependent upon a satisfactory survey, a positive response to enquiries with the local planning office and a reasonable contract, for example – it's good to express these provisions at this early stage to avoid any confusion or ill feeling later in the process. However, you're not legally obliged to proceed with the purchase until contracts have been exchanged.

On acceptance of an offer you may be asked to pay a booking deposit of a few thousand euros on account of the price of the property in order to indicate your interest – a sum that is fully refundable if completion is not reached.

However, unless there is strong interest from other buyers for the property you're looking at, this process shouldn't be necessary.

At this stage a contract – or private treaty – will be prepared in readiness for exchange. This process is co-ordinated by your solicitor, who will liaise with the vendor's solicitor. The contract should contain essential details about the property, the parties involved in the sale and the agreed price. There should also be a statement about the deposit payable on exchange, together with a date for completion within the contract.

Exchange of contracts will normally take place at your solicitor's office. At this stage you will be liable to pay a deposit – normally 5 per cent – on account of the total price of the property. This deposit remains refundable in the case of the vendor defaulting on the sale. But the agreement is binding at this juncture, so you could be entitled to sue for costs (such as those involved in commissioning a survey, retaining an architect and employing a solicitor) if the vendor does withdraw. Similarly, you could be liable for costs if you were to default on completion.

If you decide to buy at auction, you should make sure that you complete the necessary checks before the auction takes place as you'll have to sign a contract and pay a non-refundable deposit of 10 per cent of the agreed price as soon as the auctioneer's gavel goes down.

Post-completion formalities

Completion should also take place at your solicitor's office, where you will have to present a banker's draft or have transferred funds to the vendor's bank account. You will also have to pay stamp duty, which ranges from 3 to 9 per cent, dependent on the price of your property, and solicitor's fees.

You're now the owner of your property and, as such, ready to start working on your grand design.

Ireland: Context and inspiration

Ireland possesses not only a fascinating variety of relatively modern (from the Renaissance to the present day) building styles, but also a tangible heritage that goes back thousands of years. Indeed, some of its most stunning and evocative monuments belong to pre-history.

These include a wide array of examples from simple stone dolmens to large and impressive burial chambers, such as the remarkable Neolithic site at Newgrange, County Meath, which features an enormous mound surrounded by standing stones and containing a central chamber built using the corbelling technique. This technique is a method of dry-stone wall construction, which survived as a means of building primitive shelter for many thousands of years and which can be seen in a number of other surviving structures, such as the much more recent beehive huts on Skellig Michael, County Kerry. Iron Age forts, such as the particularly impressive examples on Inishmore Island – redolent of mystery and ancient superstition – are other notable prehistoric remnants to be found in a number of places.

RIGHT
The Mount Fuji-like peak of Croagh Patrick dominates the coastline of County Mayo.

Church Architecture

Precursors of more modern styles – and indications perhaps of more modern thought – are to be found in early ecclesiastical architecture that began with the foundation of Christian monasteries in the fifth century. But although Christianity in Ireland dates back to this juncture, surviving examples of church building are a great deal more modern due to the fact that churches only began to be built in stone from around the ninth century. It was at this time that rectangular church buildings first began to appear in Ireland, and many were built in the following centuries. An idiosyncratic feature to a large number of these were tall round towers – one example can be seen at Kilmacduagh in County Galway, where the towers were built over 30 metres tall. But in the main, these churches were simple stone rectangles that, in comparison to much European church architecture, were fairly primitive.

It was only in the twelfth century that Continental styles really began to pervade Irish church building, leading at first to the construction of cruciform, Romanesque and generally southern European-type churches. Following Norman incursion, the Gothic style gained supremacy and a number of cathedrals were erected, including St Patrick's in Dublin, now the national cathedral of the Anglican Church of Ireland.

The Republic of Ireland's history from this time is one of a brutal struggle with outside forces and within itself. Catholic suppression began in earnest under Henry VIII's rule of Britain and Ireland, and only really ended just over 400 years later with the foundation of the Republic in 1949. Consequently, while church architecture in Catholic countries in the rest of Europe took on Renaissance and then baroque forms, Irish Catholics barely saw the erection of a single place of worship for centuries. It wasn't until 1815 that a major Catholic building was constructed in the form of the neo-classical St Mary's pro-Cathedral of Dublin. But it was the Catholic Emancipation Bill of 1829 that really paved the way for a swathe of church building that, on both sides of the religious divide, embraced the nineteenth-century Gothic revival. And this era not only saw a surge in Catholic church building, but also one from the Protestant Church of Ireland as well.

During the twentieth century the architect Liam McCormick has perhaps been the one outstanding exponent of church architecture, designing modern, contextual buildings, such as St Aengus' Church in Burt. This is a church with a long, spectacular and – dare I say it – sensuously sweeping roof, with a circular plan that allows a window to stretch around the entirety of the building and let light flood into the interior.

Church conversions have become increasingly popular in Ireland in the last ten years, though they have not reached the levels of popularity that they have in Britain. But it's possible to see both homes and restaurants in a number of towns and rural locations that began their lives as places of worship.

RIGHT
The resurgence of Gothic architecture in the nineteenth century coincided with a massive church-building programme by both the Protestant and Catholic churches.

LEFT
Church towers may provide a wonderful opportunity for taking in Ireland's impressive scenery but creating internal access and introducing large enough windows in a sympathetic style can present a challenge.

ABOVE
Getting away from it all. There is plenty of peace and tranquillity to be found on the western coast of Ireland. It is also one of the most romantic landscapes of Europe.

Westport,
Co. Mayo

there. So we've built this box inside it that's
independent and can be ripped out fairly easily,
leaving the structure behind.' It's this particular
innovation that indicates most clearly the
sensitivity with which Andrew has approached
the building. He has a strong feeling that the
original structure should, as far as possible,
remain intact, and that any alterations have the
potential to be removed at any point in the
future. The solution in this instance was to create
a timber-framed internal structure that would be
loosely attached to the inside walls of the church

by means of soft metal ties. Only in one place,
where a balcony on the mezzanine floor extends
over the living room, is there a more rigid
attachment, where a small steel support has
been moulded into the wall. This reluctance at
wholesale intervention is also evident in the
panelling that has been inserted to house wiring
rather than cutting it into the walls.

As you walk in through the front entrance
then, the first double-height space contains a
living room on one side and a library on the
other. As you look up from this space there is a

LEFT & ABOVE
Different aspects: the slender window and large expanse of wall are reminders of the church as Andrew and Jackie found it...

...but the wooden floors, light timber roof, balcony face and balustrades illustrate the inviting sense of modernity that they have brought to it.

A thoughtful
engagement with the
building has created a
staggering sense of
drama due to the
inherent tensions –
between old and new,
austerity and warmth
– in the design.

ABOVE RIGHT
One of the two
en-suite bedrooms
on the first floor seen
across the 'bridge'
that spans the
double-height space
at the front of the
building. A ladder
rises into the attic
space.

RIGHT
The look-outs! The
church has so many
views – looking out
and looking in. Two
balustraded viewing
platforms set into the
tallest arch in the
building are topped
by the tower room
which surveys the
beautiful surrounding
landscape.

Useful Information

The stories of those people who've already built their grand design abroad should hopefully offer an insight into some of the potential challenges, pitfalls and benefits involved in undertaking such a project. They should also provide a fairly substantial dose of inspiration: after all, they're all people who've pursued the realization of their dreams with dogged determination.
And this in itself is admirable. How many of us have yearned for something and lacked the dedication, perseverance or willpower to make that dream tangible? But it's also hard not to feel a twinge of jealousy, isn't it? Even after the stresses and strains that some of them have gone through, they've all generally ended up with what they wanted, and often what many of us would want as well.

These end results have been achieved through vastly differing methods and varying budgets. However, if you're interested in following in their footsteps, it's recommended that you research and plan as methodically and intensively as possible. This book has tried to offer some basic practical advice as well as some inspiration but you will obviously want to conduct far more detailed research yourself.

The web has made that process far easier with enormous amounts of information available within seconds of turning on your computer. So rather than recommending other books, we've listed the following internet resources. They should provide good starting points for some of your research, though a lot of it can only be done on the ground by visiting places, talking to people and sitting down to work out what will be possible and what won't.

But whatever your grand design is, we wish you luck.

Web Resources

While every effort has been made to ensure that information for these sites is correct, the author and publisher cannot be held responsible for the content of third party sites.

www.aecb.net

The Association for Environmentally Conscious Building

www.architecture.com

The website of the Royal Institute of British Architects (RIBA), this contains an outstanding range of information and literally thousands of links to a diverse range of architecturally related sites.

www.ajplus.com

Keep in touch with what is happening in the world of architecture with the website for the *Architects' Journal* magazine.

http://www.andalucia.com/property/building.htm

Some tips for building in Spain.

www.bre.co.uk

The Building Research Establishment.

www.buildstore.co.uk

A company offering support and advice for self-builders.

www.cat.org.uk

An educational charity advocating environmentally-friendly building methods and technologies.

www.channel4.com/granddesigns

The world wide web home of *Grand Designs*.

www.cnplus.com

Keep abreast of the latest developments in the UK construction market with the website of *Construction News*.

www.earthship.org

Get more information about earthships – buildings constructed using recycled car tyres.

www.est.org.uk

The Energy Saving Trust. This is a government website with an array of tips on energy-saving methods.

www.franceguide.com

The official site of the French Tourist Board.

www.greatbuildings.com

A site of interest and, perhaps, of inspiration.

www.greenhomebuilding.com

This site offers information about environmentally-friendly house building.

www.iavi.ie

Irish Auctioneers & Valuers Institute. Contains advice on buying property and features land for sale on a searchable database.

www.italyassist.com

A company offering services for moving to Italy.

www.lowcarbon.co.uk

A non-profit making organization promoting building methods and technologies that produce low carbon dioxide emissions.

www.movetoireland.com

A quirky but comprehensive website about many aspects involved in a move to Ireland.

www.oasis.gov.ie/housing/planning_permission/building_a_house.html

Irish government advice on obtaining planning permission in the Republic of Ireland.

www.permaculture.org.uk

Permaculture seeks to work in harmony with the environment; this website provides a wealth of information on the subject.

www.segalselfbuild.co.uk

A website inspired by a pioneer of self-build in the UK – Walter Segal – that offers support and advice for self-builders.

www.selfbuildit.co.uk

www.selfbuildland.co.uk

General self-build information and features.

www.spab.org.uk

Society for the Protection of Ancient Buildings.

www.strawbalefutures.org.uk

www.strawbalebuildingassociation.org.uk

find out more about how to build using straw bales.

www.sustainable.ie

Information and features about sustainable living in Ireland.

Property Sites

For most countries there are many websites containing property and, less frequently, land for sale. We have given some examples for each country featured in this book in the **Practicalities** sections but the best way is probably to do your own search on a search engine with the specific criteria that you have (e.g. 'finca southern Spain').

Contributors' Websites

Some of the people involved in this venture also have their own websites, and with four of the builds – Puglia, Les Gets, La Creuse and Westport – you can actually go and stay in them as well as reading about them and watching them on TV. We're taking interactive to a whole new level here.

David and Leonie are running cultural and gastronomic holidays in the midst of the olive trees of Puglia. More information can be found at **www.ilcollegio.com**.

James and Nicky Dobree will be leasing their chalet to lovers of luxury and outdoor life. Look at **www.fermedemoudon.com** to find out more. Nicky's professional site is **www.nickydobree.com**.

Denise Daniel and Doug Ibbs offer a chambre d'hôte, with six ensuite rooms and optional evening meals. Find out more at **www.chezjallot.com**.

And if you fancy a holiday on the west coast of Ireland, you might think about staying in Andrew and Jackie Lohan's church. Have a look at **www.kilgallan.com**. Andrew is a partner at the firm Brazil Lohan. Their website is **www.brazillohan.ie**.

The concept behind the house near Malaga was provided by Gil's son, Matt Briffa, partner at the firm Briffa Phillips. Their website is **www.briffaphillips.com**.

Glossary of Terms

Here's a general guide to many of the terms that you may encounter. For more details on their usage, see the *Practicalities* section for each country.

France
architect · *architecte*
contract · *contrat de vente*
deed · *acte de vente*
estate agent · *agent immobilier*
lawyer · *avocat*
local authority/town hall · *commune* or *mairie*
notary · *notaire*
planning permission · *permis de construire*

Italy
architect · *architetto* or *geometra*
contract · *compromesso*
deed · *rogito*
estate agent · *mediatori* or *agenti immobiliari*
lawyer · *avvocato*
local authority/town hall · *comune*
notary · *notaio*
planning permission · *permesso*
retrospective approval of works · *condono*

Spain
architect · *arquitecto*
contract · *contrato privado de compraventa*
deed · *escritura*
estate agent · *agencia inmobiliaria*
lawyer · *abogado*
local authority/town hall · *ayuntamiento*
notary · *notario*
planning permission · *permiso de obra*

Arcade A series of arches and their supporting structures: piers or columns.

Baroque An architectural style chiefly of the sixteenth and seventeenth centuries. While following many of the rules of Renaissance architecture, it also breaks a great deal more and is highly decorative and monumental in style.

Castellation A parapet or tower with alternating indentations and raised portions which is sometimes called crenellation.

Cladding A non-structural outer skin of a building that does not carry any weight or support the building; in effect a superficial layer or finish.

Classicism A highly formal architectural vocabulary that has been highly influential in Western architecture since ancient Greece. It is characterized by its use of columns and orders (Ionic, Doric, etc.) and a stringent set of compositional rules.

Column A thin, upright structure, which may take a number of different forms, usually a supporting member in a building, though 'fake' columns with no structural function are also commonly found.

Concrete A mixture of sand, cement and aggregate, often reinforced with metal.

Conservation The sympathetic, gentle and minimal repair of old buildings.

Contractor The contractor usually bears the responsibility for actually building an architect's design. The contractor employs the workforce and sub-contracts out such specialist work as may be necessary.

Cupola Most often a dome-like structure, very often a church.

Elevation A scale drawing of the external faces of a building.

Embodied energy The amount of energy expended in the production of materials, particularly relevant in terms of the quantity of carbon dioxide used in the entire process, including transport, manufacturing techniques, etc.

Geothermal energy Energy produced from heating water in pipes that run into the earth. Geothermal energy has a major environmental benefit in that it offsets air pollution that would have been produced if fossil fuels were the energy source.

Gothic A style of architecture common throughout Europe between the twelfth and sixteenth centuries. Despite having a number of regional idioms, Gothic is generally seen to have achieved its apotheosis in the great cathedrals of northern Europe. Key features include flying buttresses, pointed (or lancet) arches, and ribbed vaults.

Loggia A roofed arcade or gallery with open sides; often at an upper level.

Modernism In architecture, modernism is characterized by the expression of the functional aspects of a building, usually resulting in bold cubic and geometric shapes. Concrete, metal and glass are the primary materials of the modernist vocabulary and its most famous pioneers are Le Corbusier and Mies van der Rohe.

Neo-Gothic/Gothic revival A renewed interest in Gothic architecture, popular in Europe in the late eighteenth and nineteenth centuries.

Neo-classicism A re-emergence of classical architecture in mainstream design in the eighteenth and nineteenth centuries.

Plan A scale drawing of a horizontal section of a building.

Project manager Someone who controls a construction project in its entirety, combining the role of the quantity surveyor with that of the contractor. They ensure that jobs are done at the right time, the correct materials sourced and the costs controlled.

Quantity surveyor The quantity surveyor, often simply referred to as a QS: estimates and monitors construction costs from the early stages of a project through to its completion.

Rafter A roof beam sloping from the ridge of the roof to the wall that supports the roof.

Rampart A defensive embankment surrounding a fort or castle, usually consisting of earth and stone walls.

Renaissance architecture A style of architecture that drew heavily on classical ideas of proportion, order and symmetry. Italy in the fourteenth and fifteenth centuries saw much of the great Renaissance architecture constructed in structures by Palladio, Bramante, Sansovino and Michelangelo.

Rococo A highly decorative form of baroque architecture and ornamentation that developed in France in the early eighteenth century.

Section A scale drawing of a vertical slice through a building.

Stud wall An internal, non-load-bearing wall made from timber frame.

Sub-contractors Sub-contractors are specialists – carpenters, electricians, stonemasons – who are recruited on to the project by the main contractor. Usually called 'subbies' in the trade.

Tower house A fortified medieval house with one of the wings raised to form a castellated tower. They are found in northern England and Ireland.

Vaulted ceiling An arched ceiling which may take a number of different forms including tunnel vault (single arch), groin vault (double arch) and tripartite vault (triple arch) ceilings.

Vernacular architecture A localized building style that uses regionally sourced materials to suit the prevalent climatic and historical conditions. It is building that has a sense of place, has evolved over a long period of time and that exists outside the formal canons of architectural design.

Index

Acknowledgements

**Many thanks to all the people who went on
the great adventure and let us watch it:
Gil and Hilary Briffa, Denise Daniel and
Doug Ibbs, James and Nicky Dobree, Andrew
and Jackie Lohan, Mark and Debbie Sampson,
Jen and Derek Ray, Howard Smyth and Janne
Hoff-Tilley, Leonie Whitton and David Westby.**

Thanks also to everyone on the *Grand Designs* team at
Talkback without whom the writing of this book wouldn't
have been possible: the producer, Helen Simpson; the
directors – Sasha Bates, Ita Fitzgerald and Christian Trumble;
the assistant producers – Tom Dalzell, Katy Fryer and Merryn
Hunter; the production team – Heidi Bell, Vicky Bennetts,
Louise Penez, Donna Rolls and Joanne Walton.

Thanks are also due to: the photographer, Tyson Sadlo;
Mathew Clayton, Channel 4, and everyone at *Grand
Designs Magazine*; the HarperCollins team – Denise Bates,
Mark Thomson, Pippa Rubinstein, Lisa John, Kevin Kosbab
and Julia Koppitz; Jane Turnbull; Cat Ledger; and the really
quite brilliant Bridget Owen (thank you for your
understanding and patience).